RACE, RACISM & CRITICAL THINKING
in the United States

Phillip A. Hutchison
California State University

Kendall Hunt
publishing company

Cover image © Shutterstock, Inc.

publishing company

www.kendallhunt.com
Send all inquiries to:
4050 Westmark Drive
Dubuque, IA 52004-1840

For Eric Aldaco

Contents

Acknowledgements

Of all the courses I took during my tenure as an undergraduate student, the one that stands out the most was the class that introduced me to the concepts of race and racism. I took special interest in the distinction the professor of that class made between "individual racism" and "institutional racism," and I recall sitting in class and realizing that I was learning information that was altering the way I perceived society and the people who lived in it—including myself. I had never considered racism to be anything more that the hateful thoughts and deeds of individuals of different racial groups against one another. The notion of racism as a "system of power" opened me to an understanding of the world that I had not previously possessed.

As I progressed in my graduate studies and later began to teach these very subjects myself, others started asking me with greater frequency what, exactly, had sparked my interest in the topic of racism. What I wrote directly above has been the primary answer I have given over the past several years. More than anything else, the study of racial issues helped explain to me the nature of the society I had grown up in. As I met and befriended students whose lived experiences were profoundly different from my own, I increasingly appreciated how race and racism were factors influencing so many of those differences. While the study of such societal factors as class, gender, and sexuality also illuminated the complexities of the world, in the particularities of my own personal lived experience, it was race that best explained to me the social reality that my family and friends inhabited. And so it became the main subject I have since pursued.

Predictably, I have accrued many debts—not just for the book itself, but for all those who have encouraged me and believed in me over the years. I thank my project coordinator, Thalia Cutsforth, for her assistance and professionalism, as well as John Coniglio for his frequent emails that helped push me forward. I am thankful for so many individuals, including but not limited to Mat and Camisha Borger, Nathan Morales and Karrie Benoit-Morales, Aaron Jackson and Ayesha King-Jackson, Mike Lizarraga, Ferdy Hernandez, Kari Cottom, Nika Mencarini,

Krisztian Molnar, Andres and LaToya Granados, Malcolm and Jill Thomas, Lexy Thomas, Erik Romo, George Chavez, Peter Georges, Steve and Michaela Engels, Rosalind Dixon, Brittany Dixon, Agustin Rodriguez, Leroy "Coco" Jones, Hank Solano, Marc Jackson, Ricardo Juarez, Shawna Basick, Junior Diaz, Joel Mendoza, Curtis and Kim Reed, Darlene Bel Grayson, Kim Buckley, Rachelle Johnson, Ato Doxey, Jorge Derramadero, Juan Carlos Mendoza, Kevin and Trae Holland, Jason and Vanessa Hill, Phil and Rita Aussem, Nathan Santa, Shaun Coupland Gross, Sheldon and Kate Brown, Luis Cervantes, Ivan Strean, Ron and Cheryl Hammer, OnTay Johnson, Jayson and Sarah Johnson, Claire Leong, Brad and Tiffany Josephs, Peter Overstreet and Cat Taylor Overstreet, Davis Nguyen, Jose Paez, and David Caldwell.

My involvement in the Educational Opportunity Program at California State University Northridge has been my great fortune. The staff, mentors, and faculty always push me to greater heights as I see their motivation to help first-generation college students achieve victory in their lives. I thank especially Jose Luis Vargas, Shiva Parsa, Glenn Omatsu, Bridget Sampson, Sean James, Lavelle Roberts, Rashitta Brown-Elize, Lizbeth de la Cruz, Jina Gonzalez, Marvin Villanueva, Frank Muniz, Edward Cobian, Joe Martinez, Sherek Manoukian, Jason Lumague, Daniel Mulato, Susana Amezcua, Alexis Moraila, Orlando Roybal, Norma Fausto, Mary Ly, Thomas Kollie, Luis Reyes, and Gary Gamble.

I am grateful to all the instructors, students, and families at Gold Medal Martial Arts in Santa Clarita, California. They have encouraged me, supported me, and put up with my chronic part time-ness. I thank especially Robert Gast, Hans Shin, Warren Goenner, Kyle Adler, Wesley Ryan, Justin Siegen, Erik Castillo, Danny Cabrera, Michelle Gast, Kerry Kardell, and Sue Kay. My martial arts family of the last twenty-five years extends further than this, and in this vein I also thank Ken Lewis, Gavin Espinosa, Jason Kivi, Freddy Bouciegues, Helen Gast, Julie Shin, Faith Foote, Joe and Marla Stark, Michael Ball, and Katie Mintz.

Lastly, I want to thank in a more extended way Teresa Williams-Leon, who taught that first class on race and racism and motivated me to pursue graduate school. I am very grateful to Mike and Kathy DeChellis, who first knew me as a bike-riding and video game-playing ten year-old. They have been a constant source of support for me in every stage of my academic career. And lastly and most importantly, my parents, Ken and Patti Hutchison, instilled in me a love for learning and an appreciation for education from the very beginning.

Introduction

Election Day 2012 was filled with the buzz of voters flocking to the polls and the 24-hour news media churning out the latest data indicating which states had sided with Barack Obama or Mitt Romney. Commentators editorialized on the meaning of the election and the implications it would have upon US politics over the next four years. As the day wore on and more precincts reported in, Obama decisively pulled ahead in the electoral college and was eventually declared the winner. As with every previous election, some of the events of that early November day and its immediate aftermath will beimmortalized and imprinted onto our national history. (And others will, inevitably, be lost to history.) Of all those events, two especially stood out for me, and I want to open with a discussion of them, as they highlight many of the themes we will be engaging in the forthcoming pages of this book.

The first event involved the publicized reaction of some whites, who responded to Obama's re-election in transparently racist fashion. On the social media site Twitter, nearly four hundred people expressed their disgust over Obama's victory. "About time we get this monkey out of office," wrote a high school hockey player in Pennsylvania. "When in doubt kick the [n-word] out," complained another individual. Some reporting on this debacle noted that many of those tweeting these offensive statements were high school students not linked to racist groups in any way.[1] Moreover, the locations of the tweets were geographically coded, and it was found that while they came from all across the country, they were concentrated in the Southern states and in states that Obama lost in the election.[2] The response to these tweets was swift and immediate. Protesting these anti-Obama messages as scandalous and shameful, media commentators bemoaned the number of Americans who had decided to openly air their discontentment in such racist ways.

The post-election Twitter fiasco conveys two lessons (among others) about racism in the early 21st Century. The first is the simple and uncontroversial observation that overtly racist people remain among us in our society. And the second involves the response of most others to these anti-Obama tweets: their reactions of outrage remind us that such blatant racism is condemned within most sectors of the country. Indeed, we live in a day and age where being called a "racist" is considered the epitome of insults. This, of course, stands in sharp contrast to the pre-civil rights era, where social mores all but required whites to treat people of color with contempt and derision. Whatever else is said of the civil rights movement of the 1960s, it thoroughly reconfigured how Americans speak and think about race and racism. Owing to the importance of the civil rights movement, I spend a significant portion of this book (in particular, chapters 3 and 6) focusing on the various changes it brought about.

The unabashedly racist tweeting that flooded cyberspace in the wake of Obama's victory was not the only race-related event that seized my attention. The other occurred during the election itself, just as it was starting to become evident that Obama was likely to be re-elected. On Fox News, conservative pundit Bill O'Reilly vented his frustration that so many Americans had chosen to cast their lot with Obama rather than Mitt Romney. O'Reilly was more explicit about "which" Americans were voting for Obama and why; as he lamented,

> The white establishment is now the minority. And the voters, many of them, feel that the economic system is stacked against them and they want stuff. You are going to see a tremendous Hispanic vote for President Obama. Overwhelming black vote for President Obama. And women will probably break President Obama's way. People feel that they are entitled to things and which candidate, between the two, is going to give them things?[3]

As expected, the responses to O'Reilly's rant covered the spectrum: some applauded him for telling it "like it is" and standing up to the liberal establishment. Others lambasted O'Reilly, charging him with unfairly stereotyping blacks and Latinos.

These divergent opinions remind us of the complexity of racial issues in the 21st Century. Unlike the anti-Obama tweets, which the overwhelming majority quickly wrote off as the drivel of hate-mongering bigots, O'Reilly's histrionics don't easily fall into the "racist" category. The challenge we encounter in formulating a judgment about O'Reilly's statements is that the specifically *racial* message he was broadcasting wasn't fully transparent. It's not altogether clear why he felt the need to advertise the probable voting patterns of blacks and Latinos in conjunction with his belief that people vote for Obama because they "want stuff." Recent history, however, does provide us sufficient context and background to make some educated assessments about the real message O'Reilly was attempting to convey.

At bottom, critiquing O'Reilly's comments requires that we zero in on his repeated use of the words "stuff" and "things." What are the "things" that blacks and Latinos want and evidently believe that Obama will provide for them? Over the past several decades, these groups (and black females in particular) have been excoriated in the mainstream press for their alleged "welfare dependency"— a dependency emanating from their inherent laziness and the belief that they are "entitled" to government handouts. As Martin Gilens argued in his well-known book *Why Americans Hate Welfare*, Americans support the concept of welfare in the abstract, but fiercely oppose welfare policies because the media has successfully typecast welfare recipients as poor people of color who abuse the system for their own benefit. Thus labeled the "undeserving poor,"[4] these groups today, according to O'Reilly, support Obama because they want "things," and the "things" they want are welfare, Obamacare, and the like. All this O'Reilly contrasted with the "white establishment," a group evidently prone to work hard, play by the rules, and not expect the government to hold their hands.

Of course, O'Reilly could have meant something different from this; after all, he didn't just come out and say "Latinos and blacks are lazy and want to live off the dole at white expense." And given the racial atmosphere we inhabit today, he *couldn't* have expressed it like this, as it would have exposed him to the same condemnation experienced by those tweeting racist comments about Obama. As we shall see later in this book, politicians today are forced to cloak their racial (and even racist) messages behind a veil of fairness and neutrality. Due to marked shifts in what most Americans consider "acceptable" speech about race, O'Reilly (and others sharing his opinions) are forced to do a balancing act: to broadcast racial messages in such a way that doesn't violate contemporary racial norms and thus would be judged as "racist."[5] Indeed, this is the key difference separating O'Reilly's fulminations with those Americans who tweeted offensive statements about Obama: we can presume that many of the same individuals endorsing O'Reilly's comments denounced those who saw fit to publicly call Obama the n-word.

The O'Reilly episode communicates an important fact about our racial world: *we live in a time of unprecedented uncertainty about the meaning of race.* It is a level of uncertainty never before experienced with the concepts of race and racism. In the centuries prior to the civil rights movement, white politicians and the general public had little reason to conceal their racism; they freely humiliated people of color in their rhetoric and discriminated against them in public policy. This is hardly to suggest that confusion over the meaning of race did not exist back in those years (for an example, see chapter 5.) But in our "colorblind," "post-racial" society of today, what race and racism mean and the way people deploy these terms is often far from obvious, as the O'Reilly incident makes evident.

This all produces a scenario in which we all know that race "matters," but we don't know exactly *how* it matters. This disjuncture sits at the heart of essentially every racial event that captures national attention. We will be visiting many such events in the pages of this book. My central purpose in those forthcoming pages is to acquaint readers with the enigmas of race and racism and to equip them with the tools to understand and analyze our racial realities today. From Hurricane Katrina to Trayvon Martin to the Jena Six, racism is constantly rearing its ugly head in our society, and the need for clarity in these matters proves greater than ever.

The chapters to come wade into a broad variety of racial debates, tackling such subjects as affirmative action, colorblindness, the death penalty, and much more. One of the primary goals of these chapters is to challenge readers and encourage them to think *critically* about these topics through the presentation of viewpoints and perspectives often left off the mainstream media map. The questions at the end of each chapter provide further avenues for critique, allowing readers to diversify their ways of thinking about these ever-contentious issues.

Chapter 1

What is 'Racism'?

Introduction

The other day, I was making my usual rounds of the news world, scanning the ever-increasing spectrum of available news sources for the relevant and key information pertaining to our rapidly changing society. In the midst of stories about North Korea's continued nuclear provocations and the latest gun control debate emerging in the wake of the tragedy in Newtown, Connecticut, I chanced upon a story that bore the following headline: "Tonya Battle, African American Nurse, Sues Michigan Hospital for Race Discrimination."

The controversy began when a white male refused to have black nurses care for his newborn child; he allegedly rolled up his sleeve to reveal a Swastika tattoo on his arm. Tonya Battle's lawsuit did not focus on the preferences of the man, but rather the hospital, because it granted his request, attaching the following note to the newborn's file: "No African American nurse to take care of baby." According to Battle's lawyers, this arrangement persisted for a month.[1]

The reactions to this incident by the general public fell into the predictable patterns of disbelief and anger, which were primarily aimed at the man who openly racially discriminated against Battle and other black nurses. Unambiguous in their outrage, nearly all condemned the Swastika-sporting man as an insolent malefactor whose beliefs belong in the racial stone age. Both this story and the responses to it provide yet another reminder that, despite all our attempts at transcending race and overthrowing the centuries-long nightmare that has been racism, it *still* haunts our society. Pervading our nation's history have been protests, wars, marches, crusades, and so much more: all aimed at eradicating racism in one form or another. Yet its foul presence remains, as the Michigan episode makes evident. Of course, this incident was simply one of countless other stories with which I could have opened this chapter, as we are daily confronted by the specter of race and the myriad ways it intrudes upon our lives and shapes our realities.

We'll be visiting several other recent stories by chapter's end, which will further illuminate the continuing dilemma of racism in the 21st Century. I want to bring up one more story in these opening remarks, as a counterpoint to the opening incident in Michigan. In March 2013, the website thinkprogress.org ran a story entitled "New York City Cop Testifies That He Was Told to Target Young Black Men." This revelation came in the context of recent hearings over New York's "stop and frisk" policy, which is "a method of searching people in which a cop is able to stop someone he or she suspects of a crime, and is able to frisk that individual if they feel that there is some justification." Suspicions of racial profiling sit at the heart of this controversy, as 85% of those stopped under this policy have been black or Latino. And at one hearing, a police officer testified that his superior explicitly told him to target black males between the ages of fourteen and twenty-one, a disclosure confirmed by a clandestine recording he had made during their interaction. ("I have no problem telling you this," the officer's superior declared. "Male blacks. And I told you at roll call, and I have no problem [to] tell you this, male blacks 14 to 21.")[2]

Taken together, these stories make clear that racism remains one of the pressing problems of our society. They highlight the ways in which racism operates on both an *individual* level as well as a *societal* level. In the scenario involving the black nurses, the actual instance of discrimination was a personal matter, of one clearly "racist" man showcasing his anti-black sentiments. But as articles analyzing this incident have noted, what occurred simply exposed what has been called the "open secret" in hospitals—"allowing patients to refuse treatment by a doctor or nurse of another race."[3] The Michigan affair, as such, was not merely an individual incident, but one taking place in a larger societal network in which such prejudiced requests are granted. (Indeed, the racial issues emanating from this event are two-tiered, as the actual source of the discrimination lawsuit was aimed at the hospital itself for having granted the man's request to not allow a black nurse to touch his newborn.)

New York's stop and frisk procedures present a similar quandary. Each time a young black or Latino male was targeted solely for his identity, he was the victim of an individual act of racism. But the racism itself functions on a societal level, producing a pattern in which 85% of those undergoing stop and frisk procedures were black or Latino. And this pattern emerged in the context of over five million individual instances. And unlike the indignation aimed at the white male who refused to allow black nurses near his newborn child, the practice of racial profiling gains the tacit approval of many Americans. What gives such behaviors life (and *justification*), and how can we seek to combat and eliminate their existence? Even attempting to address these questions subjects us to the sheer complexity of racial issues in 21st Century society.

This complexity demands the need for a theoretical framework, one which outlines the contours and dimensions of racism. In this way, we can better understand why racism remains such a force in the US—why it contains such "staying power." Building on the works of many previous scholars, in this chapter I construct a framework upon which to investigate the enigma of racism and the multitude of ways it has harmed our nation and so many of its people. To help tease out these complexities, I will be addressing four questions in this chapter, the first of which is the title itself: "What is 'racism'?" I then move to three other inquiries in turn: "Who is a 'racist'?"; "What is 'race'?"; and "What is 'racial justice'?" Exploring at length these four issues will allow us to engage racial issues in all their complexity. Before we begin, however, I first provide a brief presentation of the specific theoretical framework I will be employing throughout this chapter.

The Idealist and Materialist Traditions

To facilitate our analysis of racism, I introduce here two philosophical traditions that seek to illuminate how humans interpret and interact with the world around them. These are called the "idealist" and "materialist" traditions. The purpose of this section is to overview the idealist and materialist traditions, followed by their specific application to racial issues in the remainder of the chapter. Idealism and materialism are complex philosophical doctrines with a lengthy history, and a thorough analysis of them, I should make clear at the outset, lies well outside the boundaries of the present study. My goal is simply to familiarize readers with the basics of these terms and how they can be related to the study of racial issues in today's society.

In his book, *The Meaning of Marxism*, Paul D'Amato succinctly summarizes the importance of this pair of traditions: "According to their traditional usage in philosophical writing, idealism and materialism represent the two main divergent ways of looking at the world we live in."[4] Aside from their overarching importance in the field of philosophy, the operative word in D'Amato's quotation is "divergent." The idealist and materialist traditions are vastly divergent in their outlook and understanding of the world, and these differences will become evident as we apply them to our study of racism.

"For the idealist," writes D'Amato, "the mind—or the spirit, sometimes God—is the origin of all material things."[5] Human history, from the perspective of the idealist, moves forward through the power of our minds. The ancient Greek philosopher Plato is among the best-known thinkers associated with idealism; as D'Amato notes, "Plato separated the mind from matter, and argued the former ruled over the latter."[6] This dominion of the mind was also seen to regulate notions of morality: "Ideas of right and wrong, that exist above society and above time, govern human behavior."[7] In the end, material reality only exists insofar as our minds perceive it, as that reality is itself mental. To whatever degree historical change comes about in human society, it is the result of the ideas people have come up with to shape that history.

The materialist tradition all but reverses the logic governing idealism. In the words of D'Amato, "For the materialist, all of reality is based on matter, including mental activity, which is itself a result of the organization of matter in a particular way... Minds cannot exist apart from the material world, and the material world existed long before any mind was able to experience it."[8] As opposed to idealism, there *is* a material reality that exists independent of our minds. At the heart of the materialist tradition, then, is the relationship between human beings and the physical, material reality they inhabit. Whatever ideas people hold, they emerge from that physical reality. To again quote D'Amato, "Whereas the idealist places the mind above and outside of nature, the materialist argues that the mind itself is a product of natural developments."[9]

Easily the most famous materialist philosopher in history is Karl Marx, and indeed, Marxism itself is known as "historical *materialism*." For Marx and his primary compatriot Friedrich Engels, human history has moved forward in the context of "class struggle" (which was the opening point of *The Communist Manifesto*.) Such historical changes occur in human society as a result of our struggle over material resources. In the view of historical materialism, these class struggles over material resources constitute the "base" of society, while the ideology that emerges from these struggles is called the "superstructure." Key in Marxist thought is the degree to which the material base *determines* the ideological superstructure. In other words, the base is always the primary "mover" of society upon which ideas are based (idealism generally views this relationship the other way around.) The materialist tradition goes even further, arguing that battles in and between societies that "appear" to be about ideas are actually struggles over material resources.

The key, then, is how we *apply* the idealist and materialist traditions to a spectrum of social issues. The discussion has been abstract to this point, so before we tackle our main subject of racism, let's first provide a couple of examples of these two traditions in action. When the US invaded Iraq in March 2003, a variety of different reasons were proffered (both in support and in criticism) for the purpose behind the invasion. These differences generally tracked upon idealist and materialist lines. On the one hand were the justifications given by the George W. Bush administration of their desire to oust Saddam Hussein and his tyrannical dictatorship with the goal of spreading freedom and democracy to the Iraqi people (this is the idealist rendering of events.) Those coming from the materialist tradition stressed that the invasion was ultimately a struggle over resources—in this case, oil. The fact that much of the Middle East is sitting on vast oil reserves was the source of the US's interest in the region, according to the perspectives rooted in a materialist tradition. Critics of the invasion contended that the Bush administration's talk of freedom and democracy in Iraq was merely a smokescreen for the real prize: the seizing of Iraq's oil reserves—the third largest in the world.[10]

The second example involves a social issue within the borders of the US: homelessness. In posing the question, "Why are people homeless in the world's wealthiest country?", we can provide answers that come from the idealist and materialist traditions. To return to D'Amato's argument, in the idealist view, homelessness is at bottom a "personal failing." As former president Ronald Reagan put it, "the homeless...are homeless, you might say, by choice."[11] D'Amato's rebuttal to Reagan in turn illuminates a materialist interpretation of the question of why people go homeless: "The dramatic rise in homelessness in the 1980s naturally had nothing to do with the fact that Reagan halved the public housing budget and reduced federal spending to local governments."[12] For materialism, the primary emphasis is always placed on the influence of material resources and how they fundamentally shape people's opportunities and their life prospects. Applying these traditions to racial issues will help bring clarity to one of the most pressing problems of our society.

What is "Racism"?

Ask one hundred people to define "racism," and you'll get one hundred different responses. The vast majority of them, however, will contain many of the same elements, drawing as they do on the spectrum of easily accessible resources on the subject, from the media to dictionaries. Speaking of dictionaries, the 1997 American edition of *The Oxford Desk Dictionary and Thesaurus* defines racism as the "(1) belief in the superiority of a particular race; prejudice based on this; (2) antagonism towards other races." (Its thesaurus synonyms are "apartheid" and "bigotry," and equates the word "racist" with "chauvinistic.")[13] Other leading dictionaries supply similar definitions of racism, and these all parallel the perspectives students have provided me over the years when they first enter my classes. If anything, a general uniformity exists regarding what racism "means"—a uniformity that, as I will explain here, proves too constricting to adequately illuminate the concept of racism in its entirety. My purpose in this section is to inject a dose of complexity into the topic; my analysis below aims to disrupt the common conventions that govern debates over racism by highlighting aspects of the subject that are frequently marginalized.

To achieve this, I will present two different discussions of racism—each based on the "idealist" and "materialist" traditions that I introduced in the previous section. One thing that will become evident as we proceed is that I devote noticeably more space to the materialist tradition. As one might predict, I do so because the idealist tradition adheres closely to the standard views of racism propagated in dictionaries, popular culture, and elsewhere. As we shall see, the materialist tradition conveys insights that lay outside the mainstream—often far outside. Only by engaging both perspectives on racial issues can we truly grasp the complexity of our subject—and only by engaging the complexity of our subject can we truly grasp a solution to the seemingly eternal conundrum of racism in our society.

WHAT IS "RACISM"?: THE IDEALIST PERSPECTIVE

As the above section related, the idealist tradition stresses the influence of *ideas* as central to the understanding of human history and how people relate to each other. Applying this idealist tradition to the concept of racism can yield a variety of insights about what racism "is" and how it functions in society. We can thus present the following description of racism from the idealist tradition: *The problem of racism is primarily a problem of racial prejudice*. For our current purposes, the key word in this description is "prejudice."

Certainly, there are many words related to "prejudice" that are strongly associated with the idealist tradition: discrimination, stereotypes, intolerance, hatred, ignorance, bigotry—and the list goes on. The idealist tradition is thus concerned with both attitudes and the actions that flow from them. I privilege the concept of prejudice here because I view it as an effective catch-all term that covers the rest, as it is sufficiently broad and inclusive. Moreover, the reach of prejudice extends even further than we may realize, especially in light of the increasingly acknowledged observation that prejudice can operate *unconsciously*, an issue I explore at length in chapter 7. From prejudice, then, emerges the litany of contemptible behaviors that are the manifestations of racism. Such behaviors run the moral gamut, from a white person calling a black person the n-word to the extreme of committing murder in the name of race (one recalls, for example, the 1998 killing of James Byrd, Jr., a black man, by white men who tied him to the back of their truck and dragged him to his death.)

Citing prejudice as the primary problem of racism commits one to viewing racism in certain ways. Scholars, for example, often employ the phrase "racism as a set of attitudes" in describing the concept from an idealist angle. Under this reading, racism occurs because people possess the wrong attitudes towards other racial groups (and sometimes their own.) And if prejudice is the primary motivating force behind racism, it also implies that racism is an *individual* issue. It is the racism of one individual against another as it takes expression in prejudice, discrimination, hatred, stereotyping, and so forth.

Viewed in this manner, racism presents itself as a moral failing in human society. Racism is, at bottom, a matter of the heart, and to be prejudiced against others simply because they "look different" represents the epitome of that moral failing. As is often said today, there is only one race—the *human* race. The idealist tradition highlights the fact that we are all the same underneath: that our only differences are superficial in nature. Racism intrudes on society when people mistreat others solely because of these superficial physical distinctions.

WHAT IS "RACISM"?: THE MATERIALIST PERSPECTIVE

Moving to the materialist tradition will allow us to consider racism from an angle that is quite divergent from the one provided by the idealist tradition. The materialist tradition, as aforementioned, focuses on the relationship between people and the physical environment they inhabit. Approaching the issue of racism in this way produces a variety of other insights regarding how it manifests in society.

The materialist description of racism turns out to be exactly the same as its idealist counterpart, with the exception of the last word: *The problem of racism is primarily a problem of racial inequality.* That last word, of course, makes all the difference; while the idealist tradition views racism as prejudice, the materialist tradition places racial *inequality* front and center as the primary problem of racism. Rather than being a "set of attitudes," the materialist tradition conceives of racism as a "system of power." In this latter instance, racism is not chiefly about individual prejudice; rather, racism operates on a larger, societal level.

What, specifically, is racial inequality, and how does such inequality manifest itself in society? As a "system of power," racism functions as a set of *unequal power relations* based on race. In other words, it is to say that certain racial groups wield more power than other groups—they possess more economic resources, greater political influence, and so on. As a result of these unequal power relations, the *life chances* between racial groups are starkly different from one another.

Let's present some specific examples of these differences in life chances, for this is how racial inequality takes form in society. The case of housing represents a vivid example of racial inequality, as it expresses itself in multiple ways. For instance, residential segregation remains rampant in our society, with whites and people of color often living in separate areas. Yet these areas differ not simply in geography, but neighborhood quality, with whites more likely to reside in safe, resource-rich suburbs and other wealthy communities (such as Beverly Hills in Los Angeles), while people of color inhabit decaying inner cities at much higher rates. Racial inequality in housing also appears in rates of homeownership, with whites more likely to own their homes (about 75% of white families own their homes; for people of color, this figure hovers around 50%). Such inequalities extend to homelessness, with blacks living on the streets at a greater frequency than other racial groups. The existence of racial inequality, according to the materialist tradition, constitutes the primary form of racism—its very presence means that racial injustice remains in our society.

These racial inequalities materialize in essentially every measurable outcome in the nation. Income: on average, for every dollar that a white person makes, a person of color makes seventy cents. Prison rates: while blacks and Latinos represent roughly 25% of the US population, they comprise about 75% of those behind bars. Education: blacks and Latinos disproportionately attend underfunded inner-city schools and drop out at much higher rates than whites and Asian Americans (and education represents one crucial exception, as it is Asian Americans who dominate, an issue I analyze in chapter 3.) Health care: different racial groups have unequal access to health care, such that white males on average have a life expectancy that is six years longer than black males. Jobs: whites are more likely to hold more powerful and influential positions in companies, while people of color are, in full contrast, more likely to be unemployed.

We could present countless other examples here. Suffice it to say that racial inequality reaches into every crevice of society; in the above ways and more, the life chances of racial groups in this country remain profoundly unequal. Several important points follow in a deeper assessment of these racial differences. The first is the simple fact of such inequalities; at some level, we *know* that they exist. We may not be able to cite detailed statistics, but few are completely unaware that certain racial groups live in nicer areas while others go to jail more often. From our upbringing to the media, racial inequality seeps into everyday life in ways that are anything but hidden.

Since racial inequality is both visible and obvious, it begs the question of *why* such inequalities exist in the first place. Such an inquiry takes center stage in a materialist outlook on racism. It is one thing to acknowledge the "fact" of racial inequality—but completely another to take the next step and inquire of the reasons for those inequalities. A big part of the challenge that we face today is that society often answers that question for us. As Elizabeth Anderson asserts in her book, *The Imperative of Integration*, "Confronted with evidence of massive racial inequalities, Americans often explain them by invoking contemptuous stereotypes of blacks as lazy, stupid, ignorant, violent, and criminal."[14] Such stereotypes form the backbone of the justifications many give for why blacks drop out of high school and land in prison at higher rates than whites. James W. Loewen fashions a similar point in *Lies My Teacher Told Me*: "On average, African Americans still have worse housing, lower scores on IQ tests, and higher percentages of young men in jail. The sneaking suspicion that African Americans might be inferior goes unchallenged in the hearts of some blacks and many whites."[15] As before, such inequalities are explained away through reference to toxic stereotypes. In short, we see the evidence of racial inequality everywhere in society, and as Anderson describes it, we attach *meanings* to those inequalities. If blacks and Latinos dwell in slum tenements in inner cities, the story goes, it must be a function of their laziness and criminality. Such justifications for racial inequality have dominated the discourse on race since the 1960s civil rights movement, as I will discuss in chapter 3.

The materialist tradition, to be sure, emphasizes other explanations for the existence of racial inequality—ones that do not lead down the road of the "contemptuous stereotypes" that so often become the way Americans account for the presence and persistence of racial disparities. To highlight these alternative explanations, I want to analyze one more example of racial inequality—specifically, differences in *wealth* between racial groups. An examination of racial wealth inequality will allow us to entertain another—if less popular—answer to the question of why inequalities inundate the racial landscape of the US.

We must first ask, What is "wealth," and how does it differ from income? Unlike income, which is measured in the dollar amounts one takes home every month or year, wealth is concerned with the ownership of assets. Often referred to as "net worth," wealth is defined as assets minus debts (and thus it is possible to have negative wealth, which means that you owe more than you own—a situation known as being "in the red"). One's wealth is bound up in a variety of areas—stocks, bonds, deeds, 401(k)s, and so forth. The primary source of wealth, however, is found in the home, and for the average family, roughly half of their wealth is located there.[16] (As pointed out above, since whites own their homes at greater rates, we can already begin to sketch the outlines of the racial wealth gap.)

Because of these particular qualities, wealth possesses the capacity of being passed down from one generation to the next—specifically, through *inheritance*. Scholars of wealth continue to be at odds over how much of an average family's wealth has been inherited, with many estimates ranging from 50–80%.[17] Yet even lower figures can underemphasize the power of wealth inheritance; as Melvin Oliver and Thomas M. Shapiro argue, the influence of inheritance becomes more evident when it is expanded to include not simply wealth passed down upon the death of older family members, but gifts given during the life course as well (for instance, parents helping their adult children purchase their first home by giving them the down payment.)[18]

With this context in place, we can inquire of the specific figures of racial wealth inequality. I provided the data on racial differences in income earlier: for every dollar a white person makes, a person of color makes seventy cents. The difference in wealth levels, however, proves exponentially greater; for every dollar of wealth a white person owns, a person of color owns ten cents. In other words, there is a *ten-times wealth gap* between whites and people of color. Over the past twenty-five years, scholars have taken a special interest in racial wealth inequality, arguing that wealth exerts a much greater influence than income upon the life chances of racial groups.

Two scholars of racial wealth inequality, Heather Beth Johnson and Thomas M. Shapiro, have performed ethnographic studies that demonstrate the power of wealth in shaping the life chances of Americans today. From their work emerges a term, "transformative assets." These are assets that have the ability to transform a family's circumstances, helping them move to a nicer neighborhood with better schools, among other benefits. Not all inheritance is transformative in nature; it is one thing to inherit three hundred dollars, but completely another to inherit a home worth three hundred thousand dollars. In only the latter case are transformative assets at work. Predictably, as Johnson and Shapiro show, whites are significantly more likely to receive transformative assets, which has (in Shapiro's words) "allowed them to live in houses in neighborhoods that they simply could not have afforded without parental wealth."[19] This is how wealth centrally differs from income, as one can use wealth to *leverage* other advantages, a point to which I will return in a moment.

One crucial fact to stress about inheritance is that it is *unearned*. People cannot work for an inheritance; they receive it because they happen to be part of families who have wealth to pass down. In light of this fact, Shapiro coined a term to highlight the undeserved nature of inheritance: "wealthfare." Shapiro deploys this term as a counterpoint to "welfare," which continues to be a subject of great debate and opposition (due to the widespread belief that welfare recipients are lazy and wish only for the government to provide them unearned benefits.) The concept of wealthfare is designed to remind us that the inheritance of wealth is every bit the "handout" that welfare is seen to be. In the following passage, Shapiro writes of the discoveries he made while interviewing white and black families, finding that what often separated white success and black hardship was the possession of wealth—or lack thereof.

> As I spoke to families in different cities, I became increasingly aware of the profound difference between those who have a tremendous head start in life because of their family wealth and those who struggle just to obtain opportunities for themselves and their children. I believe that if we are to discuss inequality and personal responsibility we must put forward an intellectual, political, and moral distinction between families who better themselves by means of their own achievements and merits and families who move up because unearned, often inherited, advantages have been passed along.[20]

Until we bring wealthfare into the debate Shapiro makes clear in this passage, the conversation remains incomplete. While blacks are commonly excoriated in the press and elsewhere for their welfare dependency, a balanced argument must also include the fact that many whites are "wealthfare dependent," moving further ahead in life than would otherwise be possible without inheritance. Recalling the introduction to this book, this is precisely the context that is missing in Bill O'Reilly's assertion that folks who vote for Barack Obama do so because they want "things" (that is, such undeserved benefits as welfare). An argument rooted in the materialist tradition would stress that folks who vote for Mitt Romney do so because they *also* want "things" (for instance, tax policies that will ensure their inheritances remain undisturbed). Just as O'Reilly accused Obama's devotees as feeling "entitled" to welfare and the like, Shapiro and Heather Beth Johnson's research shows that wealthfare recipients carry the same sense of entitlement for their unearned benefits.

The matter of inheritance brings us to what is arguably the most important point regarding racial wealth inequality: that in order to understand disparities in wealth, *we have to look to history*. Since inheritance constitutes such a significant portion of the source of wealth, it means that such wealth has been transferred from prior generations. And if state-sponsored racism dominated US society during those prior generations, then we can appreciate why the wealth gap between whites and people of color is so large. As George Lipsitz asserts in this vein, wealth "is almost totally determined by past opportunities for asset accumulation, and therefore is the one figure most likely to reflect the history of discrimination."[21] Differing levels of wealth owe much to the past, and only by looking there can we arrive at an accurate answer to the question of why racial wealth inequality exists. To put this another way: if a nation has had centuries of slavery, Jim Crow, and other forms of legal racist oppression, it's going to leave a *legacy*. And as Lipsitz pointed out above, that legacy makes its deepest mark in racial wealth inequality.

Highlighting the "history of discrimination" is vital to understanding why inequalities characterize the racial terrain of the US, and it provides a powerful corrective to how Americans often interpret them—through reference to the "contemptuous stereotypes" that Elizabeth Anderson referred to earlier. Looking racial history squarely in the eye will allow us to see the roots of racial inequality in the countless racial policies of the past that unambiguously and unabashedly benefited whites at the direct expense of people of color. Every chapter of this book focuses at least in part on the history of racism with these precise issues in mind; I spend much of chapter 2, for example, analyzing various housing policies from the 1940s and 1950s that go far in illuminating the sources of both racial wealth inequality and contemporary residential segregation (as well as how these two are closely linked). We will see how whites were granted unimpeded access to the expanding suburbs of this era, while people of color were systematically and legally blocked from these same suburbs. This situation allowed whites to amass unprecedented wealth in the form of homeownership, which (as Shapiro noted above) became the basis of much of the "parental wealth" of which many whites are currently the benefactors.

From the above, it is clear that racial history continues to heavily influence society and the racial inequalities that contaminate it. In these discussions and others, I take my cues from James W. Loewen, who writes that "Without causal historical analysis, these racial disparities are impossible to explain."[22] I would actually attach one word to the end of Loewen's statement: Without analyzing the impact of racial history, these disparities are impossible to explain *correctly*. Because as noted above, Americans do provide explanations for racial inequality. Since the majority of these explanations do not take the history of racism into account, they usually end up latching onto "contemptuous stereotypes" that function as justifications for continued white privilege and nonwhite disadvantage.

If anything, the forthcoming chapters will make clear that the ten-times wealth gap should not surprise us in any way. The legacy of past racial discrimination remains with us in many forms, from the condition of America's inner cities to the racial imbalance in our prison system. But that legacy manifests most strikingly in racial wealth inequality, as wealth can be used to leverage other advantages—just as wealth poverty profoundly limits the options of families who do not possess it. With wealth (and especially with transformative assets), a family can move to a nicer area with nicer schools where drugs and gangs are less of a threat. This increases the likelihood of their children securing a good education, which leads to a greater rate of entering and graduating from four-year universities. Armed with college degrees, they are in a better position to land high-paying jobs. Between the strong income and the eventual inheritance, these children can then pass down these advantages to their next generation.

The wealth-poor confront notably different circumstances. As Thomas M. Shapiro found in his interviews of black parents, no matter how badly they wanted to provide the best education for their children, their lack of wealth functioned as a blockade that tethered them to inner-city neighborhoods with underfunded schools and the perennial threat of crime and drugs. In both cases, the presence or absence of familial wealth becomes a major factor in shaping the fates of families and the opportunities they can provide for their children. As Daniel Rigney notes in this vein, "Inheriting assets tends to facilitate the accumulation of further assets with each succeeding generation, while the absence of inheritance tends to beget intergenerational poverty."[23] Such inheritance-prompted asset accumulation (or lack thereof), it is crucial to stress, operates independently of an individual's desire to succeed.

Racial wealth inequality, as is evident from the above, has a hand in many of the other racial inequalities we've discussed in this section. While many today profess hope for the eventual fading away of racism and racial inequality (via inter-marriage, the ascendance of high-profile people of color such as Barack Obama, and the like), data on wealth paints a more sobering picture, as all the indications are that racial wealth inequality is getting *worse*, not better.[24] The recent wave of home foreclosures, discussed in chapter 7, will help us appreciate how the racism of the past continues to generate disadvantages for the myriad wealth-poor people of color in the US today.

HIGHLIGHTING THE CYCLICAL RELATIONSHIP BETWEEN PREJUDICE AND INEQUALITY

In the remainder of this section, I want to step back and assess the twin forces of racial prejudice and racial inequality—specifically, by focusing on the relationship between them. Prejudice and inequality are hardly mirror images of one another; after all, one is an action, while the other is a state of being. In terms of racism, however, they form an organic whole, as they mutually reinforce and feed off each other. If, for example, whites are prejudiced against blacks and Latinos because they consider them intellectually inferior, such prejudice is given confirmation by racial inequality: in this case, by the data that shows that blacks and Latinos score lower on IQ tests and drop out of high school more often than whites. These inequalities supply the *evidence* upon which prejudice is rationalized.

This process becomes endlessly cyclical. The example of racial profiling on our nation's highways illustrates this cyclical relationship between prejudice and inequality. If blacks and Latinos get pulled over more often while driving by police who suspect they are carrying drugs, such prejudice is excused away by reference to the overwhelming presence of these groups in prison because of drug-related charges. As the reasoning goes, the police *should* profile blacks and Latinos in light of this data. For this part of the cycle, the prejudice (profiling) follows the inequality (prison rates). The result of such racial profiling practices ushers in the next part of the cycle. Since blacks and Latinos get targeted for drug raids and searches, they inevitably get caught in possession of drugs more often (sociologists define this inevitability as a "self-fulfilling prophesy"). Despite all the evidence that no racial group (ab)uses drugs at significantly higher or lower rates, such racial profiling causes blacks and Latinos to get pulled in to the nation's overcrowded prison system on drug-related charges far more often than whites. And the inequality that results justifies more racial profiling—continuing the cycle.[25]

The section of the cycle I've emphasized with the materialist tradition, of course, is how prejudice becomes justified by inequality; such inequalities form the basis of those "sneaking suspicions" that such stereotypes as black intellectual inferiority may actually be true. Racial inequality becomes the soil upon which prejudice germinates—prejudice that remains all around us, from following certain racial groups around in department stores to the popular example of a woman clutching her purse more tightly (or crossing the street) when she sees a black man coming her way. Daniel Rigney further illuminates the dynamics of this cycle in a passage worth quoting at length:

> Minority disadvantages in education, employment, and the like feed white stereotypes of minority inferiority, justifying discriminatory practices that deepen these very deficits. A vicious cycle is thus set into motion, in which racist beliefs among dominant groups perpetuate minority deprivation by diminishing minority opportunities, and minority deprivation is then interpreted as further confirmation of racist beliefs. In the absence of intervention to break this vicious cycle, the disadvantaged become more disadvantaged.[26]

It is this "vicious cycle" that makes tackling racial inequality enormously difficult, for reasons that will become clearer in the forthcoming chapters of this book.

The cyclical nature of prejudice and inequality explains why I went to the trouble of attaching the word "primarily" to my descriptions of racism ("The problem of racism is *primarily* a problem of racial prejudice or inequality."). For each tradition, both prejudice and inequality matter; they simply underscore opposite ends of the cycle. The idealist tradition does not necessarily discount the matter of racial inequality—it just views inequality as *secondary*. The same holds true of the materialist tradition: prejudice still matters, but it is relegated to secondary status. As I explained above, for the materialist tradition, the root of racism is racial inequality—and prejudice is merely a *symptom* of it.

In the final analysis, vast differences separate the idealist and materialist traditions in their views of racism. These differences were first put on the table a half a century ago by Stokely Carmichael and Charles V. Hamilton in their celebrated text, *Black Power*. In the following quotation, they use the term "individual racism" to refer to the idealist tradition and "institutional racism" to refer to the materialist tradition:

> When white terrorists bomb a black church and kill [four] black children, that is an act of individual racism, widely deplored by most segments of the society. But when in that same city—Birmingham, Alabama—five hundred black babies die each year because of the lack of proper food, shelter and medical facilities, and thousands more are destroyed and maimed physically, emotionally and intellectually because of conditions of poverty and discrimination in the black community, that is a function of institutional racism. When a black family moves into a home in a white neighborhood and is stoned, burned or routed out, they are victims of an overt act of individual racism which many people will condemn—at least in words. But it is institutional racism that keeps black people locked in dilapidated slum tenements, subject to the daily prey of exploitative slumlords, merchants, loan sharks and discriminatory real estate agents.[27]

Note again the difference between prejudice and inequality that emerges from this passage: they contrast the "act" of individual racism with the "function" of institutional racism. Likewise important is the greater level of destructiveness Carmichael and Hamilton associate with the materialist tradition: while the act of racial terrorism that killed the four black children is surely to be condemned, the institutional conditions that resulted in the deaths of five hundred black babies should receive an even greater outcry. Racial inequality, of course, forms the bedrock of their ruminations, as white babies were much less likely to die from such conditions as malnutrition and lack of access to medical care.

Whatever label we attach to these distinctions—prejudice v. inequality; individual v. institutional racism—they constitute profoundly divergent ways of interpreting the concept of racism and how it operates in society. The three forthcoming questions I pose in the remainder of this chapter ("Who is a 'racist'?";

"What is 'race'?"; "What is 'racial justice'?") will be informed by the insights I have shared in this section. As was the case here, our answers to these questions will end up looking quite different depending on whether we approach them from the idealist or the materialist tradition.

Who is a "Racist"?

At first glance, the response to the question "Who is a 'racist'?" might not appear to be worth spending an entire section addressing. The answer seems so obvious. However, because I am analyzing these issues from two points of view—the idealist and materialist traditions—I will actually be providing two answers to this question: answers that differ on every fundamental level. The discussion thus becomes more complicated than it appears on the surface. And we'll also be entertaining another, directly related question, one that continues to invite controversy today: Can only whites be racist? Collectively, our replies to these two inquiries will allow us to access deeper insights regarding the complexity of racism itself.

WHO IS A "RACIST"?: THE IDEALIST PERSPECTIVE

Let's apply our discussion of racism from the idealist tradition to the matter of racist people. If the problem of racism is primarily a problem of racial prejudice, it follows that racist people are those exhibiting such prejudices and their concomitants (discrimination, ignorance, hatred, stereotyping, etc.). If this represents the "obvious" answer, it merely exposes which of the two philosophical traditions dominates our thinking about race and racism today.

That the idealist tradition generally governs our views of racism should scarcely surprise us; indeed, overt displays of racial prejudice and hatred are the "contact points" of racism, ones that cannot but produce visceral reactions for anyone involved directly or indirectly. Predictably, Hollywood movies that cinematize racial issues (*American History X, Crash, The Help*, and so forth) foreground these aspects of racism precisely because of the emotions they evoke. This directly relates to the kind of horror we feel when (recalling the example from Stokely Carmichael and Charles V. Hamilton provided earlier) a white racist bombs a church in Birmingham, killing four innocent black girls. In this instance, it is clear who the "racist" is, and few would debate the moral disapprobation that should be visited on anyone who acts in such a vile manner.

Viewed in this way, it stands that a member of any racial group can be a perpetrator of racism—or its victim. The deleterious consequences of racial hatred can fly in any direction—indeed, from this perspective, one can even be prejudiced against one's own racial group. Racial prejudice and hatred, in the idealist tradition, are not the sole province of whites.

When we move to the materialist tradition in regards to these issues, however, we shall see that they are anything but clear-cut.

WHO IS A "RACIST"?: THE MATERIALIST PERSPECTIVE

How (and where) do racist people figure into the materialist tradition? Since the focus centers on racial inequality, the profile of a "racist" doesn't immediately appear to fit. Again drawing on Stokely Carmichael and Charles V. Hamilton's example from above, when five hundred black babies die every year in Birmingham "because of the lack of proper food, shelter, and medical facilities," who is the "racist"? Their deaths were not the direct result of actions by individuals. These difficulties require that we take a slightly different approach than we did with the idealist tradition. As such, my purpose here is to establish the *relationship* between racist people and racial inequality, and in so doing, some entirely different—and possibly unexpected—insights will emerge.

We can begin by focusing on one particular inequality I held to be of special importance: the ten-times wealth gap between whites and people of color. As aforementioned, much of this chasm owes to the much greater likelihood for whites to receive unearned bequests in the form of inheritances, which Thomas M. Shapiro labeled "wealthfare." These sorts of benefits contrast sharply with its counterpart, welfare. When Bill O'Reilly and other right-wing pundits fulminate against welfare, they've picked a visible target to assail. This is because welfare is a *public* policy, a part of the government budget. It is obvious how much of it is being spent to fund these welfare programs.

Wealthfare fundamentally differs from welfare on this very point. Unlike welfare, which involves the public transfer of public expenditures, wealthfare (and wealth in general) is *privately* passed between generations. As Heather Beth Johnson points out, in contrast with welfare, which is open and visible, intergenerational transfers of wealth "are normally hidden from public view," with their advantaging effects thus flying beneath the radar.[28] Furthermore, people can inherit any amount of wealth—up to and including "transformative assets"—regardless of their racial attitudes. That is, members of the Ku Klux Klan have the same potential to become the recipients of wealth inheritance as do whites who are antiracist. The very nature of wealth as a private possession (as opposed to the public nature of welfare) allows to be transferred in ways fully independent of what they think or feel about people of color.

Thus we arrive at a key insight: *racist individuals are not necessary for the perpetuation of racial inequality.* As seen in the above contrast between wealthfare and welfare, wealth represents an especially clear example of this: the intergenerational passage of transformative assets will occur, whether people behave in "racist" ways or not. This insight is concisely captured by the sociologist Eduardo Bonilla-Silva, who asserts that "the intentions of individual actors are almost totally irrelevant to the explanation of social outcomes."[29] Racist people can certainly exacerbate racial inequality, but on balance, such inequalities will persist in their absence. For the intergenerational transfer of wealth, no racist intervention is necessary.

The title of Bonilla-Silva's book, *Racism without Racists*, further highlights this point. From the idealist perspective, the title doesn't make sense: how is it possible to have "racism without racists"? Acknowledging that Bonilla-Silva is approaching his topic from a materialist viewpoint (signaled by the book's subtitle, *Color-Blind Racism and the Persistence of Racial Inequality in America*) renders his title perfectly intelligible and sensible. We cannot have "racial prejudice without racists," but "racial inequality without racists" is the reality we face today.

These points are further echoed in an important passage from philosopher Charles W. Mills's essay, "Racial Exploitation and the Wages of Whiteness": "In talking with the white majority," he avers, "the imperative task has usually been to convince them that, independently of whether or not they are 'racist' (however that term is to be understood), they are the beneficiaries of a system of racial domination and that *this* is the real issue, not whether they have goodwill toward people of color or whether they owned any slaves."[30] It centrally implies that our focus on rooting out racist people is ultimately misplaced; while we can collectively feel vindicated when society rebukes such popular figures as Michael Richards and Don Imus for their public displays of racist vitriol,[31] this does next to nothing to address (let alone remedy) the fact that black and Latino children are more likely than white children to go to bed hungry. While most agree that racist behavior is morally reprehensible, ridding the nation of racist bigots will not in itself eradicate racial inequality.

In light of the above, we can return to the related query: Can only white people be racist? It's a trick question of sorts, since the focus of the materialist tradition is not individuals, racist or otherwise. The solution to the puzzle lies in Charles W. Mills's passage above: independent of their racial feelings, whites "are the beneficiaries of a *system* of racial domination" and will receive privileges from that system, from the higher probability of receiving inherited wealth to not being followed around in a liquor store. And importantly, all this will happen whether whites like it or not. So, in this sense, racism *is* a "white" issue, since it is whites who benefit on a systemic level. And many of these benefits emerge because whites dominate the institutions where racial inequality thrives, from the political system to the media to Fortune 500 companies.

In this vein, we might also consider the support of policies that, while race-neutral on the surface, serve to maintain racial inequality. One such policy is the "estate tax"—the tax on inherited wealth. As I argued earlier, Bill O'Reilly's paeans against welfare ignore such policies as the estate tax, which recent Republican administrations (in particular, George W. Bush) have sought to heavily reduce if not abolish. The elimination of the estate tax prevents the government from meddling in the inheritances the wealth-rich will either receive or pass down to the next generation.[32] And while the estate tax is not itself a racial policy, eliminating it ultimately helps keep racial wealth inequality intact because whites have exponentially more wealth to transfer to their next of kin; indeed, it is what allows "wealthfare" to have the degree of influence that it does. These "practices of racial inequality," as Imani Perry calls them, can be loosely applied to the idea of racist people in the context of the materialist tradition.[33] In the end, however, it still takes individual people to support such policies as the estate tax—individuals who would never consider themselves as "racist" for having done so.

What is "Race"?

The above analyses of racism and the dilemma of "racist" people have been more fully illuminated by scrutinizing them from two divergent angles—what I have termed here the "idealist" and "materialist" traditions. Here, we turn to the idea of "race" itself and again apply these two frameworks as a means to sharpen our understanding of this prickly and polemical concept. As evidenced by the title of this book, race and racism are not the same thing, and it proves important to flesh out their unique characteristics.

Over the years, it's been common for students to furnish dictionary definitions of race and racism in their journals. As our earlier discussion of racism made evident, I find the dictionary to be profoundly limited in its ability to tackle these concepts in all their complexity (to say nothing of the fact that they often present these concepts as if only the idealist tradition existed). To address these limitations, this section presents two definitions of race as rooted in each tradition. I break down each definition and mine them for further discernment regarding these matters. As we shall see, while both definitions emphasize different aspects of the race concept, they are largely compatible with one another and help to construct a more complete picture of "race" than that provided by dictionaries.

"RACE": THE IDEALIST DEFINITION

As per usual, we begin with the idealist tradition. The idealist definition of race reads as follows:

> *A socially constructed way of dividing human beings based on some sort of physical appearance.*

Let's examine the constituent parts of this definition in turn.

The first part of the idealist definition of race stresses its status as a "social construction." In short, race is a human invention: far from representing an eternal attribute of humanity, "race" as we conceive it today has only existed for the past three to four centuries.[34] As a socially constructed human invention, then, race possesses no biological basis, despite attempts over the past several centuries on the part of anthropologists and other scientists who attempted in vain to provide evidence of significant genetic differences between racial groups. The notion that a biological reality underlies the race concept remains popular,[35] but the view of race as a social construction represents the current dominant perspective.

Social construction or not, the idealist definition of race then highlights its role in *dividing* human beings. Race has never functioned as a means to bring people together in unity and harmony. From the beginning, the whole point of the race concept was to manufacture unbridgeable chasms between members of different racial groups—and to get these groups to say to each other "you are not like me, in any way." This produces what philosopher Lawrence Blum has termed "moral distancing"—the idea that if two individuals are not of the same race, they must have nothing in common.[36] Even a cursory glance at US history will reveal the truth of race's existence as a tool to divide human beings—and a sobering reminder of how effective a tool it remains today.

But how does this division specifically take place? Race is not the sole fault line separating individuals; religion, gender, class, nationality, and sexuality are just some of the ways people have segregated themselves throughout history to the present day. Here, race's distinguishing characteristic is its obsession with the physical—that is, the phenotypical characteristics etched on to different human bodies. Despite its fixation upon the physical, race only focuses on certain aspects of such difference ("*some sort* of physical appearance"). We "racialize" such features as skin color, hair texture, and eye shape, and these three arguably represent the primary means by which we demarcate the various racial groups today. Other somatic qualities, in contrast, lie outside the orbit of race; for instance, we don't "racialize" the shape of a person's ear, or whether or not one has an attached earlobe. The very fact that we "racialize" particular qualities of physical appearance and not others becomes one of the many salient signs that, at bottom, race is a socially constructed figment of the imagination.

Since the civil rights movement, many have insisted that since race has no basis in reality, it should therefore be ignored in government and society (this is the "colorblind" view examined more fully in chapters 5, 6, and 7). One common rejoinder to this argument draws on sociologist W. I. Thomas's famous dictum from nearly a century ago: "If men define situations as real, they are real in their consequences." Thus, while race has no roots in biology, it still possesses a *social* reality—in a word, we live in a society where people believe that race indeed exists, and they act on that belief in their everyday lives. The consequences of those actions—protracted across centuries—imbue the concept of race with a social reality that has proven enormously difficult to transcend. That difficulty sources from the fact that, as we observed earlier in this chapter, this reality is material in nature. To account for that material reality, we need a second definition of race, one that helps illuminate the *reasons* we divide people upon racial lines in the first place.

"RACE": THE MATERIALIST DEFINITION

Many aspects of the materialist definition of race flow logically from our earlier discussions of the materialist tradition itself.

A socially constructed way of transferring resources and opportunities from one group to another, camouflaging the unfairness in that transfer.[37]

Whatever their points of departure, the idealist and materialist traditions both conceive of race as a human invention and as an instrument to divide people. The first important divergence between the two involves the *kind* of division that results. The idealist definition, while emphasizing race's divisive properties, in no way commits one to the conclusion that such division necessarily produces superiority and inferiority. In other words, simply "dividing" people doesn't necessarily imply that different racial groups occupy higher or lower rungs in society. It could be that individuals of various racial groups are simply that: "different," but in no way of greater or lesser intrinsic worth or moral value.

However, as this materialist definition of race makes clear, such division has been stratifying to its core. Under this reading, race operates as a lens that channels resources and opportunities away from one group (in this context, people of color) and towards another group (white people). We label "racism" the actual processes by which these transfers have taken place in the US and beyond, policies producing the myriad racial inequalities enumerated earlier in this chapter. Physical differences, which are central to the idealist definition of race, become simply a means to that end. That is, the physical markers that lie beneath the concept of race become the determining factors vis-à-vis who will benefit—and who will suffer—from the transfer of resources and opportunities that race makes possible.

Yet race does not simply create and furnish the social conditions for these transfers to take place: it also makes them *seem fair*. As psychologists and others have demonstrated, no one wants to think of herself or himself as a bad person. So it is with larger systems of oppression: from slavery to colonialism to the Holocaust, every system of oppression has been *justified*. Race becomes an ideal means by which to take heinous acts of barbarism and cast them into feats of virtue and grace. In the name of race, cruelty transforms into purity, and malice morphs into propriety.

The history and consequences of slavery provide a vivid and grim illustration of how the materialist definition of race has operated in US history. In slavery, we clearly witness the transfer of resources and opportunities away from blacks and toward whites. In many respects, blacks *created* those resources as they labored endlessly for the material betterment of their white masters and American society as a whole. And in creating those resources, slaves also created opportunities for whites (whatever their immigrant or class status) to pursue and possibly achieve the "American Dream." As Stephen Steinberg points out regarding this very issue, "the wealth that flowed from slavery had a great deal to do with the expanding opportunities for those early Americans who exemplified Puritan virtues of industry, frugality, and prudence."[38] This perspective thus establishes the *symbiotic relationship* between white privilege and nonwhite disadvantage; it was not merely the case that whites received opportunities and blacks were enslaved—rather, it was that whites received opportunities *because* blacks were enslaved.

What distinguishes American slavery from previous forms of slavery was its *racial* character: all slaves were black. How, specifically, did slavery's proponents justify the practice? Unsurprisingly, racial ideology was central to its success. By socially constructing differences between (in this case) fair-skinned Europeans and dark-skinned Africans, an assemblage of racial myths emerged, which posited Africans as savage, brutish "sub-persons" whose inherent moral degeneracy made slavery their ideal station in life. Religion played a significant role in buttressing such racist logic, as evidenced by the "curse of Ham" story that began widely circulating during this time. (This fable distorted the biblical story of Ham, who was cursed by his father Noah for an act of transgression; according to the racist revision, the specific curse Ham received was "black skin.")

The relationship between racial slavery and religion was captured in a famous quotation by the French philosopher Montesquieu, who asserted in 1748: "It is impossible for us to suppose these creatures [black slaves] to be men, because, allowing them to be men, a suspicion would follow that we ourselves are not Christian."[39] Such was the genius of inventing "racial" distinctions: by placing blacks into the category of the subhuman ("three-fifths of a person" in the words of the Constitution), it allowed whites to treat them in ways that flagrantly violated the Christian command to "love thy neighbor as thyself." It permitted whites to deprecate and vilify blacks and other people of color—conduct that would be considered incontestably immoral if directed at other whites. At bottom, the establishment of the color line legitimizes behavior that would otherwise be considered abhorrent and un-Christian.

As the abolitionist movement gathered steam in the decades leading up to the Civil War, those supporting slavery scrambled to fabricate new justifications for its preservation. In what became one of the most popular rationalizations, apologists for slavery countered the abolitionists in insisting that—far from being a pernicious, un-Christian practice—slavery was *good* for the slave. In this reworked racist folklore, white Europeans had rescued blacks from "a life in the bush" in Africa; if anything, slaves should be *grateful* for slavery, since it gave them the opportunity to be exposed to the "civilizing" influence of whites.[40]

Thus we witness the various components of the materialist definition of race at work, as a means of transferring resources and opportunities from people of color to whites, while making the whole process appear ethical and just. "Race" is all about taking superficial physical differences between human beings, and *making those differences matter*. This gets accomplished by assigning fictitious values to these differences (in contemporary parlance, we call these "stereotypes"). Under this reading, variations in physical characteristics are merely the external indicators of deeper, more meaningful differences: for example, the light skin of whites is the outward mark of chastity and superior moral character; and the dark skin of blacks signifies their savagery and intellectual inferiority. Second-class citizenship becomes the sensible location for members of the latter group. In the end, this all *justifies* what is at bottom a massive redistribution of wealth and opportunities, enriching those classified as "white" at the direct (and symbiotic) expense of those classified as "others."[41]

One of the primary questions that will concern us as we move forward in this book is, How is racial inequality justified *today*? In the early 21st Century, few among us would even distantly defend the practice of racial slavery, to say nothing of the other legal practices pockmarking US history (Jim Crow, Japanese American internment, and the forced relegation of Native Americans onto reservations, to name a few). As we shall see, central to the complexity of race and racism today is the conspicuous (and celebrated) lack of legal barriers to opportunity. Since we no longer encounter "No Mexicans Allowed"-type signs or other racist obstacles, how then does our society rationalize the continued presence of such entrenched inequalities as the ten-times wealth gap?

Before we address these questions squarely, we do need to tackle one final issue: in light of all that has been discussed in this chapter, what does "racial justice" ultimately look like? And what needs to be done to achieve it?

What is "Racial Justice"?

In his 2001 book, *The World Is a Ghetto*, sociologist Howard Winant traces the centuries-long history of the crusade for racial justice; from the earliest manifestations of race-based oppression, countless people have fought and died to eradicate racism in all its forms. In US history, some of these battles are well-known, from the Civil War to the civil rights movement. Almost all of us are familiar with Martin Luther King's thunderous proclamations from his famed "I Have a Dream" speech, in which he yearned that his four children would one day "live in a nation where they will not be judged by the color of their skin, but by the content of their character."

The quest for racial justice continues today, if in decidedly altered forms. Our nation has battled against and victoriously vanquished slavery, Jim Crow, and a host of other racial evils. Despite all these triumphs, the specters of racial inequality and racial prejudice continue to plague our society today. Any campaign to attain racial justice must take into account the unique contours of our nation, from the presence of overtly racist individuals and groups (such as the Ku Klux Klan) to the conviction held by many Americans that talk of racial justice is superfluous, since it has already been achieved thanks to the toppling of legal racism in the civil rights movement.

In light of the above, this final section assesses the outlines of racial justice from the idealist and materialist traditions. In each case, we entertain two interrelated questions. First, *what* would need to be done to obtain racial justice in the US; and second *how*, specifically, do we go about achieving it?

WHAT IS "RACIAL JUSTICE"?: THE IDEALIST PERSPECTIVE

What would racial justice look like under the idealist tradition? As we've discussed above, the primary problem of racism is that of prejudice according to this tradition. And if prejudice is the problem, then the solution follows naturally: eliminate the prejudice. The idealist tradition views racism as a "set of attitudes"; as such, racial justice entails a readjustment and reformation of one's attitudes towards other racial groups. Since the idealist tradition conceives of racism as an individual matter, the solution must operate on an individual level.

With this in mind, how do we specifically achieve racial justice? Many programs are already in existence to address racism from an idealist angle, and they all fall under the umbrella of *education*. The point is to educate people out of their prejudices, helping them see that the individual attitudes they hold of other racial groups are often misguided and the result of stereotypes. From there, the idea is to get people to stop mistreating others on the basis of race.

One of the most widespread mechanisms designed to produce an idealist version of racial justice is known as the model of diversity and multiculturalism. Under this model, instead of belittling others because they are "different," the goal is to appreciate those differences. Groups have unique perspectives and ways of life, from food to music to outlooks on the world, and far from dividing each other based on such cultural differences, we should strive to *celebrate* them. The idealist tradition, as we've seen throughout this chapter, insists that racial groups have equal moral worth. Racial justice involves the *recognition* of that equal worth through an affirmation of our differences and how they form the diverse tapestry of our nation.

A bevy of programs have sprouted up to mitigate racial problems that emerge in the workplace and similar settings. Variously called "sensitivity training" and "tolerance training," such programs encourage racial amity by bridging the divisions that often exist. For instance, a high school located in Anaheim, California had been hosting a "dress like a Mexican day" for several years. Following complaints from students (when, predictably, many came to school adorned in stereotypically offensive garb), the event was cancelled and, as reported by the *Los Angeles Times*, school administrators were required to "undergo diversity and sensitivity training."[42]

Such incidents are more commonplace than they might appear, especially on college campuses. Every few months, another story rolls in of a fraternity or sorority hosting a racially themed gathering, such as "gangsta" parties in which white students dress up in blackface, wearing gold chains and drinking forty-ounce bottles of malt liquor—all the while encouraged to behave in a stereotypically "ghetto" fashion. In one recent situation in late 2012, members of the Nu Gamma chapter of the sorority Chi Omega at Penn State University held a Mexican-themed party, from which a controversial photo surfaced online. In the photo, over two dozen sorority members donned ponchos and sombreros and carried signs that read "Will mow lawn for weed and beer" and "I don't cut grass, I smoke it."[43] Even more recently, in February 2013, members of a fraternity at Duke University threw a party entitled "Kappa Sigma Asia Prime," where guests came dressed as geishas and wore conical hats. (The party invitation read, "We look forward to having Mi, Yu, You and Yo Friends...over for some sake.")[44]

When these parties evoke outcries for being racially insensitive and offensive, the participants usually express surprise and befuddlement at the negative reactions. Seeming completely oblivious to all the racial lines they cross when they dress and act in such manners, they often dismiss the criticism by claiming that others are "oversensitive" and need to learn "how to take a joke."

Whatever reasons are supplied for their racially questionable behavior (and whatever the sincerity of those supplying them), the idealist solution remains the same: reforming attitudes through education. This choice of approach becomes clear when we catalog the response of university administrators and others to these parties and the negative publicity they generate. For example, in response to the Penn State Mexican-themed photo, the sorority began working on "educational directives" for the members who were involved. And at a protest of the "Racist Rager" fraternity party at Duke, Asian Student Alliance President Ting-Ting Zhou argued, "This protest is about the destructive prejudice that must be uprooted from every corner of Duke to make this place an inclusive and safe place for all."[45] Again, the motifs of "education" and "diversity" have a prominent place in the reactions to these racially-charged parties and how to deal with them. If "racism" is a function of these various expressions of prejudice, it follows that transcending racism involves targeting such prejudice and expelling it from society.

WHAT IS "RACIAL JUSTICE"?: THE MATERIALIST PERSPECTIVE

Considering how divergent the idealist and materialist traditions have been as evidenced throughout this chapter, it should come as little surprise that in questions of racial justice, the materialist tradition leads us into another realm entirely—a realm where the implications for racial justice become—almost by definition— decidedly more radical (and decidedly less popular, as we will see). Stating the goal is the only simple step: if racial inequality is the cornerstone of racism itself, then racial justice would entail the elimination of those inequalities. The gaunt racial differences we see today in income, education, life expectancy, prison rates, wealth, jobs, and so forth would have to be swept away. From this point of view, the very fact that (for example) the infant mortality rate for blacks is significantly higher than for whites represents just one expression of a wrong that would have to be rectified in order for racial justice to be realized in this country.

The radical implications for racial justice stem primarily from the fact that the conversation moves from people's attitudes (the idealist tradition) to the social structure (the materialist tradition). While the prescriptions for the reforming of people's racial attitudes have been generally embraced, the proposed plans for the attainment of racial equality have been met with sentiments ranging from trepidation to outright hostility. Dissolving racial inequality presupposes large-scale alterations in the very structure of society; if racism occurs on the institutional level, any antiracist reorganization of society must take place on that level (as opposed to the idealist proposals for eliminating racial prejudice, which are individual in nature). For the materialist tradition, racial injustice exists because the life chances between racial groups remain starkly different.

The actual fulfillment of racial equality has proven to be nothing short of elusive, since, as noted above, proposals designed to create such equality have been met with fierce opposition—especially on the part of whites. We see this opposition manifest in the debate over the one policy that has made some inroads in society, one which has attempted to combat racial inequality head-on: affirmative action. I devote an entire part of this book (chapter 4) to a study of affirmative action, and we will analyze the details of the policy itself and the nature of the profound resistance it faces. My extended focus on affirmative action emerges not because it is a "great" or "unfair" program, but rather because it forces us to confront racial inequality and the historical legacies of racism responsible for bringing it about.

Whites' notorious antipathy towards affirmative action and related (if less well-known) programs has produced one of the central quandaries facing researchers who study racism and racial attitudes in the post-civil rights era. The overwhelming majority of whites today profess a belief in the *principle* of racial equality; they place their confidence in Thomas Jefferson's words in the Declaration of Independence, that "all men are created equal." The dilemma for scholars of race and racism is this: while most whites agree with the principle of racial equality, many of these same whites *oppose every program designed to make that principle a reality*. Affirmative action represents a premier example of such a program; despite their support for racial equality in principle, the actual construction of racial equality (in *practice*) has produced antagonism on the part of whites, many of whom interpret such attempts as "reverse discrimination" or "racism in reverse" (see chapter 4).

The road to achieving racial justice has thus been (and will continue to be) rocky; the following chapters of this book will help to explain why, by referencing the sources of white enmity to programs designed to dispel racial inequality. Much of this centers on the many ways these racial inequities are *justified* today, as pointed out in the previous section. If, for instance, blacks "deserve" their racially unequal status, opposition to policies intending to improve their status logically follow.

The materialist tradition's emphasis on creating a racially equal society exposes the shortcomings of its idealist counterpart. As discussed above, many today tout the value of "diversity" in securing the goal of racial fairness and justice. From the more radical standpoint of the materialist perspective, the adoption of "diversity" appears limited and conservative in its ability to address the problems that racial inequality presents to our society. Indeed, there are only certain aspects of diversity that we celebrate—language, food, clothing, music, and so forth. Other manifestations of diversity (for instance, diversity in prison rates or life expectancy) fall completely off the radar.[46]

This problem is compounded by the fact that our fixation on these nonpolitical expressions of diversity takes the focus off the racial injustices plaguing today's society. Celebrating diversity creates the illusion that Something-Has-Been-Done to improve race relations, when from the materialist viewpoint, by many measurements, racial inequality is worsening, as in the evidence of a racial wealth gap that is widening rather than shrinking. The diversity/multiculturalism model would have us hold hands and ride off into the racial promised land sunset. But when it comes time to unclasp our hands and return home, who will go to the gated community in the suburbs? And who will return to the drug-infested slum tenement? So long as a racial dimension exists in our answers to these questions, racial injustice remains.

In the end, the materialist tradition communicates to us the radical implications of attaining racial justice. *From the materialist perspective, racial justice is not achieved when we all decide to be nice to each other. Racial justice is achieved when we no longer live in a nation where white males live, on average, six years longer than black males.* Since these various forms of racial stratification continue to define our society, our ideals of racial justice remain out of reach. My central purpose in the forthcoming chapters, then, is to help us better understand why racial justice remains an unrealized attribute of our society. Much of that understanding centers on illuminating and examining the obstacles that stand in racial justice's way, guided by the conviction that we can only overcome such obstacles if we comprehend them fully.

A materialist outlook on racism in society also considers the impact of prejudice. Earlier in this chapter, we discussed the *cyclical relationship* between racial prejudice and inequality; we noted that prejudice is justified through reference to inequality (for instance, the stereotype of black and Latino males as criminally minded is given confirmation by racial inequality in our nation's prisons and jails). Achieving racial justice from the materialist perspective thus implies the following: get rid of racial inequality, and prejudice will disappear with it, *since the basis for the legitimation of prejudice has been removed.* Of course, this assertion is impossible to empirically verify, since we've never had anything approaching racial equality in our existence as a country.

At multiple junctures throughout this chapter, I've pointed out that the insights produced by the materialist tradition are notably less popular than those offered by its idealist counterpart. These prescriptions for racial justice force a commitment far outdistancing anything most Americans are willing to make, as reflected in their opposition to the policies designed to produce racial equality in our nation. Because of that opposition, one could argue that defenders of the racial status quo have an *interest* in embracing and advancing the idealist tradition's emphasis on individual racial prejudice, as doing so safely takes the focus off not only racial inequality, but the history of white racism that created it. Calling everyone to "tolerate" others' differences and celebrate "diversity" becomes the comforting antidote to the much greater commitment the materialist tradition would require to achieve racial justice. It communicates to great effect why a perspective on racism grounded in the materialist tradition has proven to be less popular in our society.

Conclusion

One of the prime difficulties hampering any analysis of racism is the presence of widespread disagreement over what it means and the influence it has upon our lives. Mainstream society has sidestepped that disagreement by concentrating on only one aspect of racism—that which falls under the idealist tradition. By conceiving of racism as merely a function of the bad attitudes people hold towards one another, the material privileges whites possess in our racially unequal society go unscrutinized and unchallenged.

In this chapter, I brought forth an analysis of racism from two perspectives: the idealist tradition (which largely parallels the standard outlook on racism) and the materialist tradition (whose points of view go largely undiscussed). I made little attempt to camouflage my conviction in the explanatory superiority of the materialist tradition; I have found it to bring forth a more accurate reading of the nature of the racial differences that daily surround us. Focusing on racial inequality as the primary problem of racism goes further than an analysis of racial prejudice in helping illuminate the current racial circumstances we find ourselves in.

Another reason the materialist tradition proves useful in highlighting racism is that it takes the focus off of "good" and "evil" people and places it where it arguably belongs: the social structure. The concept of the "black tax" exemplifies this very point. The black tax refers to the higher amounts blacks (on average) pay for the same situation, such as in housing. If there are two identical homes next door to each other with the same asking price, and a white family purchases one home and a black family the other, the black family will end up paying more. Because of racial wealth inequality, the white family is more likely to have wealth to use as a larger down payment, which reduces their monthly mortgage and the overall interest they will ultimately pay.

The key is that what produces this situation *is fully disconnected from racial attitudes*. The two families could become best friends, with children on the same soccer team. No idealist-type "racism" need occur for the white family to get the better end of the deal, and no "racist" real estate agents are necessary. Despite all this, the black tax remains in effect, as the black family will struggle comparatively more to make their higher monthly payments, and all other things being equal, they will face a variety of disadvantages the white family will not, from a higher risk of foreclosure to less disposable income (since more of it is going towards paying the mortgage). As scholars have shown, due to differences in wealth, black families are in relatively precarious circumstances, as they are more likely to be one paycheck away from poverty. The materialist tradition's emphasis on racial wealth inequality helps us understand the greater struggles families of color face due to a lack of inherited wealth; as a result, Barbara Ehrenreich and Dedrick Muhammad note, "when an African American breadwinner loses a job, there are usually no savings to fall back on, no well-heeled parents to hit up, no retirement accounts to raid."[47] Thus, white families' comparatively secure footing also leads to less stress, since they are more likely to have wealth that can help them weather economic storms. A study of racism that focuses solely on racial prejudice and bigotry will be unable to account for such issues as the black tax and the way it differentially affects (in this case) whites and blacks.

The chapters to come will continue to provide further details on these racial situations. As expected, the materialist perspective dominates throughout; while I will scrutinize racial attitudes, I am chiefly interested in institutional racial inequality and its effects upon the racial order in this country. We begin with the policies of the New Deal and the formation of suburbia in the mid-20th Century. Taking a materialist approach on these subjects will help us identify the roots of many of the racial inequalities that define our society in the 21st Century.

Questions

Before you read this chapter, were your views on racial issues more closely aligned with the idealist tradition or the materialist tradition? Has it changed? Why are idealist perspectives on racism more mainstream than their materialist counterpart?

How do prejudice and inequality relate to one another? In what way(s) are they in a *cyclical* relationship?

I spent much of this chapter analyzing the concept of *wealth* and why it is so important to understanding racial inequality today. Why is wealth a better indicator of racial inequality? How is wealth used (or, as I put it, "leveraged") to gain access to other advantages?

One important distinction I made in this chapter was between "welfare" and "wealthfare." How are they similar? How are they different? Why is the overwhelming majority of attention in the mainstream press focused on welfare rather than wealthfare?

At several points in this chapter, I mentioned that white wealth and nonwhite poverty were linked *symbiotically*. What does this mean?

Larger philosophical question: are we trapped by our circumstances/ victim mentality?

In this chapter, we discussed the estate tax: the tax on inherited wealth. Should inherited wealth be taxed? How high should the tax rate be? Is it "racist" to want to eliminate the estate tax?

Imani Perry recently introduced the idea of the "practices of racial inequality." Where else might we see these practices in action?

Do you think the ridding of inequality would cause prejudice to disappear too? Why or why not? Do certain forms of prejudice operate outside the boundaries of inequality (media, families, etc.)?

I argued that eliminating inequality will also precipitate the eradication of prejudice. Could this happen the other way around—could the removal of prejudice from society also produce the elimination of inequality?

I placed "education" under the idealist tradition's strategy to achieve racial justice. How might education also be a part of a strategy on the part of the materialist tradition?

Chapter 2

White Privilege and Nonwhite Deprivation in the New Deal Era

Introduction

The previous chapter introduced us to a variety of racial inequalities: income, education, wealth, jobs, and myriad others. There, I entertained the question of *why* these inequalities exist in the first place, since they cannot exist due to random chance. In this chapter and those following, we'll be intensively studying out some of the primary answers to this question that individuals and groups in the United States provide. While chapter 1 was chiefly concerned with racial theory, my focus in the forthcoming chapters is to provide more specific details from both history and the contemporary era.

Many scholars and others today contend that in order to understand why racial inequality manifests in so many areas of US society, we must look to history—a point we visited in chapter 1 when we discussed racial wealth inequality. In other words, the *roots* of these inequalities are to be discovered in the legal racism that pervaded the US prior to the civil rights movement, of which slavery and Jim Crow are the best-known examples. Because of such racism in the past, these individuals maintain, whites have inherited advantages that continue to privilege them today—while nonwhites have inherited a wide variety of disadvantages that prevent the playing field from being truly even.

The pursuit for slave reparations (providing monetary compensation to the descendants of former slaves) is one such campaign guided by the belief that the racism of the past—in this instance, slavery—represents the principal source of contemporary racial inequality. First initiated by Congressman John Conyers (D-Michigan) in 1989, the slave reparations bill has been axed every time it has shown up for debate in the House of Representatives. Whatever its previous (or future) fate, the struggle for slave reparations is animated by the conviction that the political and economic challenges blacks face today is the direct legacy of slavery. Organizations such as The National Coalition of Blacks for Reparations in America (N'COBRA) have taken great pains to emphasize how the legacy of slavery remains among us today in the form of higher black poverty rates, the concentration of blacks in crime- and drug-infested inner cities, and so forth.

Over the past several decades, academic historiography has painted a clearer picture of the historical roots of contemporary racial inequality, strengthening the claims of N'COBRA and other groups. While such research has indeed established robust linkages between slavery and black economic hardship, it has also suggested that we don't have to look nearly that far back to locate the roots of the countless racial inequities that blanket our country today. Many historians have identified the "New Deal Era," a period spanning from roughly the mid-1930s to the mid-1970s, as fundamental to the creation of many of the material racial differences we experience today—including the ten-times wealth gap analyzed at length in the previous chapter. As such, the primary purpose of this present chapter is to identify those aspects of the New Deal which have played an important role in creating 21st Century racial inequality.

In our study of the policies of the New Deal, we will observe the materialist definition of "race" in action; we shall see how these policies enriched whites and financially denuded people of color. The resources made available by the New Deal were gobbled up disproportionately by whites, from old-age insurance (Social Security) to prime neighborhoods in the suburbs, which exploded in size and influence during this time period. Leaving people of color out of most of these opportunities for resource accumulation thus made more of those resources available for whites than for which they otherwise would have had access. And in being left out of (for instance) the resource-rich suburbs, people of color fell prey to other exploitative mechanisms that only served to make their economic prospects more and more precarious.

This chapter first examines the New Deal itself and explores how people of color were systematically denied most of the largesse made available by its policies. We then move to an analysis of the roots of contemporary racial segregation, which took form during this era, one known as "white flight to the suburbs"; this chapter will discourse at length on the processes that facilitated this flight as well as the accompanying quandary of those left behind in the decaying central cities. As indicated above, our purpose here is to demonstrate how the collective consequences of these policies form the basis for many of the racial inequalities enveloping US society in the 21st Century.

A New Deal...for Whites

While the US today continues to attempt to break out of the "Great Recession," it is the Great Depression of the 1930s that remains the foremost economic crisis in our country's history. As the breadth and depth of this infamous catastrophe became evident, the federal government was placed under increasing pressure to intervene in the economy and restore the vitality of the market. The "New Deal" became the primary means by which to make that attempt. Whether it was the New Deal or the US's entry into World War II (or some combination thereof) that actually caused the country to climb out of the chasms of economic calamity remains a subject of fierce historical debate. My intervention in this section will not settle that debate, but rather will focus on the racial dimensions of these New Deal policies: specifically, those elements which allowed whites to reap most of its benefits.

One complicating aspect of the programs of the New Deal was their race-neutrality. Every New Deal policy was "colorblind"; that is, none of them made any reference to race in their provisions. It should be known, however, that these policies would have openly excluded blacks and other minorities had it not been for the 14th Amendment's "equal protection of the laws," which forbade any explicit racial distinctions in federal programs. The story of how people of color were largely excluded from New Deal benefits becomes a lesson in itself: a lesson in how simple it was to circumvent the inconveniences of the 14th Amendment. Despite that inconvenience, determined whites would easily unearth ways to hamper the prospects of people of color by any means possible. (We witness an earlier example of this with the 15th Amendment, which gave black males the right to vote—in this instance, whites created such technically colorblind loopholes as the "grandfather clause" and literacy tests to disenfranchise blacks—as well as poor whites.)

What political historians label the "Solid South" proved central to this process. The South voted as a Democratic bloc—every time. Since President Franklin Delano Roosevelt was also Democratic, he had to win the South's approval for any New Deal policy he wished to pass. Since the white South's credo was, essentially, "We would rather starve than see blacks gain equality," they made sure that New Deal policies heavily favored whites. Political historian Ira Katznelson highlights one of the primary methods by which they accomplished this in spite of the racial obstructions imposed by the 14th Amendment; as he describes it,

> whenever the nature of the [New Deal] legislation permitted, [the Solid South] sought to leave out as many African Americans as they could. They achieved this not by inscribing race into law but by writing provisions that, in Robert Lieberman's language, were racially laden. The most important instances concerned categories of work in which blacks were heavily overrepresented, notably farmworkers and maids. These groups—constituting more than 60 percent of the black labor force in the 1930s and nearly 75 percent of those who were employed in the South—were excluded from the legislation that created modern unions, from laws that set minimum wages and regulated the hours of work, and from Social Security until the 1950s.[1]

The Social Security Act, which Katznelson discusses here, proves a case in point. The Social Security Act covered all laborers, but the "Solid South" refused to pass it unless farmworkers and maids were omitted from its benefits. Since blacks were overwhelmingly employed in these professions, the Social Security Act effectively left out most blacks without ever having to name them, thus in no way violating the 14th Amendment.

As Katznelson implies, these sorts of maneuvers saturated the policy initiatives of the New Deal, effectively tilting its benefits toward whites. The Constitution could not block such methods, and what Katznelson describes as the "relative indifference"[2] of other political legislators ensured that the "Solid South" and its racist desires would reign.

In this, the materialist definition of race becomes active. When most blacks were barred from the resources the Social Security Act made available, it didn't cause those resources to simply disappear: those resources were obtained by whites instead. "Race" functions not simply as a means to "take away" resources and opportunities from people of color; it is *also* about transferring them to whites. The racial restrictions of the New Deal guaranteed that whites would get a "better deal" not simply because they were white—but because blacks and other minorities were systematically left out of it.

The same arguments could be made about housing. The New Deal era was also the era of what urban historian Dolores Hayden calls the "sit-com suburb," which witnessed an unprecedented expansion, particularly in the years following World War II. As we explore the sources of present-day residential segregation, we will also come to better understand the presence of the durable wealth gap that continues to stubbornly separate the fates of whites and people of color.

"Chocolate Cities" and "Vanilla Suburbs"

The formation of present-day suburbia owes much to the Home Owners' Loan Corporation (HOLC) and the Federal Housing Administration (FHA), established by President Franklin Delano Roosevelt in the early years of the New Deal era. These agencies—which were essentially liaisons between the federal government and the banks—gave an unparalleled number of families the chance to become homeowners. They helped kickstart the homebuying process that remains generally in place today: thirty-year mortgages with manageable down payments and interest rates. As the construction of new homes in the suburbs accelerated at a dizzying pace, more and more American families began to move away from the central cities. And the overwhelming majority of the families gaining access to this new, prime real estate were white. How did this come to be, and how were the HOLC and the FHA involved?

In this instance, the HOLC and the FHA were beholden to one of the dominant real estate mantras of the New Deal era: racial homogeneity. The official mortgage underwriting manual of the FHA bowed to this mantra in no uncertain terms: "If a neighborhood is to retain stability," the manual directed, "it is necessary that properties shall continue to be occupied by the same racial and social classes. A change in social or racial occupancy generally leads to instability and a reduction in values."[3] Among other tactics, the FHA accomplished this by "color-coding" every neighborhood in the US—blue, green, yellow, and red. Areas in the blue were given fantastic mortgages and interest rates, while in "redlined" neighborhoods, the FHA often refused to underwrite mortgages at all. The racial composition of a neighborhood, as pointed out above, was one central predictor of what color a particular locality would fall under; as Thomas Sugrue writes, "The FHA regularly refused loans to black homebuilders while underwriting the construction of homes by whites of a similar economic status a few blocks away."[4] George Lipsitz provides another specific example from the Los Angeles area: "FHA appraisers denied federally supported loans in the racially mixed Boyle Heights neighborhood of Los Angeles because it was a '"melting pot" area literally honeycombed with diverse and subversive racial elements.'"[5]

Boyle Heights actually had two strikes against it; not only was it multiracial, it also fell out of another major preference category in the FHA's color-coding scheme: it was located in a central city. The first-rate housing deals—in the areas colored blue and green—were thus to be found in the monoracial suburbs. As numerous urban historians have thus asserted, the collective policies of the HOLC and the FHA all but created the modern-day white middle class. The HOLC and the FHA heavily subsidized the entry of whites into these burgeoning suburbs, helping them to secure wealth in the form of homeownership—wealth now being passed down to their (grand)children, a point made in chapter 1. As George Lipsitz notes, the sum total of the FHA's policies "channeled almost all of the loan money toward whites and away from communities of color."[6]

The above, however, doesn't answer the question of why the move to suburbia was an almost exclusively white affair. Keeping people of color out of the suburbs was accomplished through several mechanisms, the most prominent of which was the racial "restrictive covenant," an instrument employed to legally bar the entry of nonwhites in targeted neighborhoods. Buoyed by the aforementioned mantra of real estate agents (racial homogeneity), restrictive covenants formally excluded racial minorities on the title deed of the property. A restrictive covenant from Seattle was typical:

> No property in said addition shall at any time be sold, conveyed, rented or leased in whole or in part to any person or persons not of the Caucasian race. No person other than one of the White or Caucasian

race shall be permitted to occupy any property in said addition or portion thereof or building thereon except a domestic servant actually employed by a person of the White or Caucasian race where the latter is an occupant of such property.[7]

(Note, of course, that people of color were permitted in such areas, so long as they were clearly in service to whites.) Neighborhoods covered by restrictive covenants were awarded better mortgages and interest rates by the FHA and the HOLC.

Restrictive covenants were declared unconstitutional in the 1948 Supreme Court case *Shelley v. Kramer*, which I examine closely in chapter 6. Despite their demise, other strategies to prevent the entry of people of color continued to guarantee the virtual all-whiteness of suburban neighborhoods: concurring with the real estate mantra that people of color would drive down property values, many whites had unofficial, mutual agreements that they would not allow the color line to be broken in their neighborhoods.

> For years, blacks who set foot in certain working-class white neighborhoods were often beaten or harassed. Those who tried to buy had bricks hurled through their windows, their front porches burned. Blacks who made it out to middle-class suburbia endured a more refined and WASPy version of the same—indignant housewives with picket signs and a steady drumbeat of neighborly reminders that "maybe you'd just be more comfortable someplace else."[8]

Even one's celebrity could not insulate people of color from the animosity of whites, as Nat King Cole discovered when he moved into the then all white district of Hancock Park in 1948 (the Ku Klux Klan placed a burning Cross on his front lawn, and his neighbors asked him to move away).

The combined weight of these mechanisms produced a massive reshuffling of racial groups in the central cities and suburbs. This demographic phenomenon was so pronounced, urban historians began calling these areas "chocolate cities" and "vanilla suburbs." Whites fled the central cities with such haste that the racial demographics of major US cities transformed with a rapidity not experienced before or since. The Detroit metropolitan area is often identified as a textbook example of the above; while in 1940 blacks made up 9% of the population of the city of Detroit, by 1970 that figure had ballooned to 44%. That increase was made possible in part by the exodus of whites to Detroit's "vanilla suburbs" of Dearborn, Royal Oak, and other suburban subdivisions.[9] (And indeed, in 1980 blacks made up only 4.2% of the population of Detroit's suburbs.)[10]

Taken together, it is of little surprise that suburbia started out as a landing spot for white families. Granted unimpeded admission into the lavishly funded suburbs, and assisted every step of the way by the HOLC and the FHA, whites would encounter in the suburbs a treasure trove of wealth—an unprecedented procuring of assets that goes far in explaining the gargantuan wealth gap we see today. The post-World War II suburban explosion, in the final analysis, proved to be "racial" in every way. David Freund summarizes the issue in his book, *Colored Property*: "Each year between 1935 and 1960, between 78.4 percent and 84.5 percent of the nation's housing starts were detached, single-family homes, the lion's share of them privately owned in suburban communities that remained almost exclusively white."[11] As with the Social Security Act, because whites prevented people of color from entering into suburban privilege, they artificially raised their own standing even further (in other words, many white families occupied homes that would have gone to families of color had the latter group not been denied access to them). And for those families of color systematically left out of the opportunities suburbia provided, their prospects often went the other direction.

Contract Leasing: Down the Racial Slippery Slope

The ascendance of suburbia carried with it another shift: homeownership itself became a major part of the "American Dream." The proverbial two- or three-bedroom house with the white picket fence, the manicured lawn, two children, and a dog (or a cat) became a staple of what it meant to "make it" in the US. Many black families bought into this imagery and desired to purchase their own homes as well; however, as the previous section highlighted, they were prohibited on two fronts. First, restrictive covenants and other devices kept them out of suburbia; and second, the policies of the HOLC and the FHA "redlined" the neighborhoods they remained trapped in. As such, they could not purchase homes unless they could buy them in total—a luxury few blacks possessed.

All this set the stage for the introduction of a ubiquitously exploitative real estate practice that gripped redlined central cities at the very moment whites were securing HOLC- and FHA-underwritten mortgages for their new suburban homes: a practice known as *contract leasing*. In 2009, historian Beryl Satter published her book, *Family Properties*, the first extended academic analysis of contract leasing, and my discussions of contract leasing in this chapter and others draw heavily on her pioneering work.

Briefly, the practice of contract leasing occurred in the following way: white speculators and real estate agents would first purchase homes in redlined black neighborhoods in full. Then, they would double or triple the price of the home and lease it "on contract" to prospective black homebuyers—often not telling them that they were the actual owners of the property (a convention we would today label "predatory lending"). As Satter remarks, due to redlining, black families "could not do what most whites would have done—obtain a mortgage loan and use it to pay for their property in full."[12] While a stunningly horrific deal, contract leasing was the only way many blacks could hope to own a home and participate in the "American Dream."

Contract leasing contained none of the perquisites provided to white suburban homebuyers. "Like homeowners, they were responsible for insurance and upkeep—but like renters they could be thrown out if they missed a payment."[13] And those payments proved to be exorbitant, since the price of the property had already been inflated two- or threefold. That, in addition to maintenance costs, inevitably led to many black families falling behind on their monthly payments and getting evicted from their homes. And whatever investments they had made on the home for improvement (for instance, repairing the plumbing or upgrading the patio) vanished, since the terms of the contract stipulated that the entire value of the property returned to the contract lessor. All told, contract leasing had a devastating effect on black families, systematically vacuuming out what little wealth they had going into the agreement in the first place. It thus comes as little surprise that, in Chicago alone, it was estimated that black families were losing a million dollars *every day* as a result of contract leasing. This money, of course, went directly to the white contract lessors, who reaped unimaginable profits from their exploitation of black America. And the practice was completely legal.

Conclusion

Through an analysis of the New Deal era, we can identify many of the practices that have directly translated into a host of the racial gaps we encounter today, from residential segregation to racial wealth inequality. In every instance, "race" functioned as a lens that pulled New Deal benefits and opportunities for home-ownership away from people of color and toward whites. At the very moment that the door to resource-rich suburbia opened for white families, blacks and other racialized minorities were not only stopped out, but became exposed to a spectrum of exploitative practices, not the least of which was contract leasing. The economic fates of whites and nonwhites thus sharply diverged at the very moment when the nation began leaning towards eliminating Jim Crow and other legal racist practices in the civil rights movement.

As we move to the civil rights movement in the forthcoming chapter, we shall see how these divergences set the stage for many of the challenges that civil rights leaders and the nation as a whole would face. By the time Martin Luther King, Jr. delivered his famous "I Have a Dream" speech in 1963, the residential pattern of "chocolate cities" and "vanilla suburbs" was already largely locked in place—along with all the benefits and burdens attached to them. As was the case here, my analysis in chapter 3 concentrates on the implications of the civil rights movement for racial inequality and the ways such inequalities would persist despite the elimination of Jim Crow and the ascendance of "equality of opportunity."

Questions

How do the policies described in this chapter help inform the geography of Los Angeles today, from Compton to Simi Valley to East Los Angeles to Pacific Palisades?

Why do you think racial homogeneity was so important to real estate agents and the Federal Housing Administration?

Why were whites so determined to keep people of color out of their neighborhoods in the post-World War II era?

In chapter 1, I made a reference to the *symbiotic* nature of white privilege and nonwhite deprivation. What examples do we see in this chapter of this concept?

Chapter 3

The Shifting Contours of Race and Racism in the Civil Rights Era

Introduction

In 1964, Martin Luther King, Jr. published his book, *Why We Can't Wait*, which chronicled the civil rights crusade against Jim Crow in the South in the early 1960s. King centralized the power of nonviolent direct action as a means to expose the moral bankruptcy of the Southern white racist establishment. Optimism fills the pages of *Why We Can't Wait*, an optimism forged in the successes of the early civil rights movement and the signs that further legal and social improvements in the lives of blacks lay within their direct reach. King, of course, makes clear throughout the book that he was under no illusions as to the profound resistance the civil rights movement faced at the hands of individuals and organizations determined to keep blacks "in their place." But one leaves the pages of *Why We Can't Wait* with a sense that better days were ahead: that the sacrifices of the civil rights movement were not to be in vain.

Three years later, King wrote his final book, *Where Do We Go from Here: Chaos or Community?* Early in this text, King asked a pair of questions that stood in sharp relief to the overall tone of his previous book: "Why is equality so assiduously avoided? Why does white America delude itself, and how does it rationalize the evil it retains?"[1] Needless to say, this is a pronounced shift in a short three years. As we will examine in this chapter, the three years separating these two books became a time of great uncertainty for the civil rights movement. My purpose is to illuminate and analyze the context for that uncertainty and how it altered the course of the movement, eventually leading to its demise by the mid-1970s.

There are countless studies of the civil rights movement in circulation, and my intervention here is not intended as a comprehensive history of it. Following my approach in chapters 1 and 2, I scrutinize the civil rights movement through the lens of *racial inequality*. Whether directly addressed or not, the specter of racial inequality triggered the change in tenor between *Why We Can't Wait* and *Where Do We Go from Here?* Much of my discussion in this chapter focuses on the realization by King and other leaders of the civil rights movement (as well as the government itself) that racial inequality was going to persist despite all the victories of the movement in eliminating legal racial barriers. Indeed, the opposition of whites to the actual establishment of true racial equality was what produced King's profound apprehension as communicated in the questions I quoted above. What the idea of civil rights meant for most whites was "legal racial equality and the equal right to vote, but nothing more." When blacks and their allies began protesting (and rioting) for "something more," the civil rights movement became the focus of repression (of which the assassination of King in April 1968 was simply one of the more significant moments).

As a result of this repression (and related efforts), the civil rights movement ultimately phased out without achieving thoroughgoing racial equality. Despite all its triumphs, the unfinished revolution that was the civil rights movement laid the framework for the ongoing battles over racial inequality that we face today. So much of the way we think about race and racism in the 21st Century—from affirmative action to "political correctness" to the celebration of diversity—is a legacy of the changes ushered in by the civil rights movement. No investigation of racism and racial theory can be complete without a study of the civil rights movement, and our analysis of it will provide a better understanding of the nature of today's battles and why the quest for racial justice remains incomplete.

The Historical Background of the Civil Rights Movement

If anything could be said of the civil rights movement, it is that it was not the spontaneous outburst of the marginalized for social justice. Racially oppressed people have been fighting for their rights since the invention of the concept of race (a point I raised in Chapter 1), and they have experienced periodic victories over the centuries. The Civil War of the 1860s, of course, was one watershed moment in the pursuit of racial justice. However, as I will discuss in further depth in chapter 5, that victory proved to be short-lived, for within a few decades after emancipation, Jim Crow had rooted itself in the nation's racial fabric with the same intensity that slavery had. Further agitation for racial justice remained necessary, but it was not until the post-World War II era that a confluence of forces converged that would succeed in collapsing Jim Crow and other forms of state-sponsored oppression.

While an extended examination of these forces lies beyond the scope of this chapter, it is useful to highlight some of the most important, as they help communicate why the heyday of the civil rights movement was the 1960s, rather than the 1930s, 1910s, or any other decade following the rise of Jim Crow in the late 1800s. What occurred in the post-World War II era that allowed blacks (in the words of Jack Bloom) "to alter the terms of their subjection"?[2] For instance, one would need to stress the Holocaust, whose effects rippled throughout the nation as horrified Americans witnessed the wickedness that racism could produce. The anticolonial movements in Africa, Indochina, and elsewhere in the post-World War II era also galvanized the burgeoning civil rights movement, as struggles for justice abroad inspired struggles for justice at home. Indeed, many black soldiers had themselves fought for freedom during World War II—only to continue to have those freedoms denied to them upon their return to the US.

The final precursor to the civil rights movement important to underscore here was likewise international in scope: the Cold War. As both the US and the Soviet Union sparred for ideological influence on the world stage, the Soviet Union took full advantage of the racist structure of the US and accused the nation of hypocrisy. Their message became, in short, "You claim to be the leaders of freedom and democracy, but look what you do to the people of color within your borders." In this situation, Jim Crow quickly became an international embarrassment and a liability. Racial issues turned into the "Achilles' Heel" of the country, as it was commonly described. The US government suddenly had an added incentive to begin heeding the voices of the marginalized and the dispossessed—voices that had been clamoring for racial justice from the very earliest.[3]

All these forces and myriad others laid the material and ideological groundwork for the modern-day civil rights movement; they gave the voices of those vying for racial justice an unprecedented legitimacy. As a result, the first bricks in the edifice of legal racial oppression began to give way. Many scholars target two major events that signal the initiation of the larger movement that would eradicate that edifice in full.

The first event was a court case: the 1954 decision *Brown v. Board of Education*. This decision, which I assess more fully in chapter 6, declared the Jim Crow doctrine of "separate but equal" unconstitutional. The Court's ruling, hailed today as one of the most important in US history, indicated in no uncertain terms that the US was heading in a new direction in its handling of racial issues. As was the case with virtually every civil rights milestone, commentators made reference to the implications *Brown* would have on the international stage—especially with the Cold War in full force. While *Brown* faced fierce resistance, the decision itself established that a new era—to be named the "civil rights era"—was dawning.

The second event transpired when Montgomery, Alabama NAACP secretary (and seamstress) Rosa Parks refused to give up her bus seat to a white man in December 1955, which initiated an ultimately successful year-long boycott of the city's bus system. The Parks incident, as we know, was an episode waiting to happen—there had been several previous attempts at instigating a boycott, which had later been aborted. The successful onset of the Montgomery Bus Boycott placed the indignities of Jim Crow on the national stage, and the boycotters' victories further propelled the nascent civil rights movement into a crusade wider in scope and larger in ambition than anything seen since the Civil War a century earlier. The Montgomery Bus Boycott was also significant because it was the first campaign led by the individual who would become the moral and symbolic leader of the civil rights movement in its early years: Martin Luther King, Jr.

Upon *Brown* and the Montgomery Bus Boycott, the civil rights movement had begun in earnest, with goals that started to crystallize and become reality. The sections to follow closely analyze those goals, in addition to their limitations; as we shall see, the successes of the early civil rights movement were merely a preamble to the many frustrations that would hinder and disable the movement in its later years. As will become evident, the civil rights movement was in a position to effect great change in certain areas of racial thought and policy—but at the same time, there were other areas that would remain all but impervious to critique. It is these latter areas that demand our attention, for they constitute many of the unsolved dilemmas surrounding race and racism today.

The Limitations of the Early Civil Rights Vision

With the merging of the forces and events described in the previous section, by the late 1950s-early 1960s, the civil rights movement had metamorphosed into a full-fledged campaign. The Southern wing of the movement, led by Martin Luther King, Jr., adopted the Gandhian doctrine of "nonviolence" as a means to expose the racist hatred of the white establishment. Such individuals as Bull Connor (Birmingham's Commissioner of Public Safety) came to symbolize that hatred, as he and his minions viciously opposed blacks who attempted to exercise their Constitutional rights. They employed notorious intimidation tactics, aiming high-pressure water hoses at nonviolent marchers, siccing dogs at them, and arresting them en masse.

We need to first pause and inquire of the *goal* these early civil rights protests possessed. However it expressed itself, that goal can be summed up in the phrase "legal racial equality." This is precisely what blacks and other people of color did not have at any moment prior to the civil rights movement. In the South, of course, Jim Crow segregation reigned, from separate bathrooms to being barred from restaurant lunch counters (the latter a well-known site for protest). And in the nation at large, racial discrimination was perfectly legal, from "Mexicans Need Not Apply" signs in storefront windows to official policies in universities that they would not enroll any students of color. In every sense imaginable, people of color had no legal racial equality to speak of; whites could freely discriminate against them without fear of reprisal or retribution. At bottom, this defined the early civil rights vision: the elimination of all forms of state-sponsored racial oppression, giving all Americans, irrespective of color, the equal opportunity to participate in the "American Dream."

On this score, little debate exists regarding the success of the early civil rights movement. As history records, whites (especially outside the South) were dismayed by the transgressions of the racist white establishment; with memories of the Holocaust still fresh in their minds, they began to increasingly support the goals of Martin Luther King, Jr. and his large cadre of civil rights visionaries. The government also took greater notice, and in the early 1960s, the likelihood of passing comprehensive civil rights reform increased. One of the most celebrated moments during these years was the August 1963 March on Washington, with King's "I Have a Dream" speech on the steps of the Lincoln Memorial as the centerpiece. By then, it was only a matter of time before Congress would push through the legislation that would realize the goal of legal racial equality. The assassination of President John F. Kennedy in November 1963 did little to slow the campaign for civil rights reforms. Lyndon Baines Johnson, who assumed the presidency upon Kennedy's death, had become a visible supporter of the civil rights movement and took the political lead in making the goal of legal racial equality a reality.

The predictable opposition the civil rights bills faced ultimately gave way to their eventual passage. In July 1964, President Johnson signed into law the Civil Rights Act, which made racial and gender discrimination illegal in job hiring and college admissions. Then, in August 1965, Congress passed the Voting Rights Act, which illegalized the intimidation tactics Southern whites utilized to keep blacks from exercising their 15th Amendment rights (this included the various loopholes they had introduced to nullify the 15th Amendment, such as the Grandfather Clause). Three months later, the 1965 Immigration Act was passed, which eliminated the racist immigration policies that had been in place beginning with the passage of the 1882 Chinese Exclusion Act, the first of a series of immigration prohibition acts. With these and other pieces of civil rights legislation, legal racial equality—more popularly known as "equality of opportunity"—became the law of the land for the first time in US history.

Things did not end quite so happily, however. As the above civil rights laws came closer to being passed, the *limitations* of the early civil rights vision were beginning to become more evident. "Even before the March on Washington," Leon Litwack remarks, "Martin Luther King, Jr. sensed that his dream was in trouble, that segregation was only part of an elaborate network of racial inequality in housing, jobs, income, and education."[4] Equality of opportunity was surely crucial—and obtaining it had been a significant victory—but it had equally significant limits. We can sum up these limitations thus: What civil rights leaders and others had come to acknowledge was that *equality of opportunity would not lead to equality of result*. What is "equality of result," and why would it not automatically follow in the wake of equality of opportunity?

We can answer these questions by highlighting the differences between equality of opportunity and equality of result. As aforementioned, equality of opportunity simply meant that race would not function as a barrier to jobs, universities, and so forth. "No blacks allowed" signifies the lack of equality of opportunity. Equality of result signifies something different. It is one thing to grant all racial groups the opportunity to apply for jobs—but who actually gets those jobs is another matter entirely. For equality of result to take hold in that case, racial groups would have to be hired in the same proportion as the population at large. We can further outline the contours of equality of result by describing a hypothetical city that is 80% white and 20% black. For equality of result to be the reality, if 80% of the city's population is white, then 80% of the politicians should be white, 80% of the prisoners should be white, 80% of the college students should be white, and so on throughout the city. By the same token, if 20% of the city's population is black, then 20% of the lawyers should be black, 20% of the city's unemployed should be black, 20% of the office managers should be black, and so forth. The key is that this pattern did not take hold—by any stretch of the imagination. Instead racial "*in*equality of result" (or what I've simply called "racial inequality" to this point) would persist in the nation despite the presence of equality of opportunity.

One major reason that equality of opportunity did not translate into equality of result can be summed up by the word "qualifications." A company may have stopped discriminating against blacks in compliance with the 1964 Civil Rights Act, but simply because blacks could now apply did not mean they would actually get hired (and quite frequently, they didn't). While old-fashioned racism was surely at work here, in many cases, blacks were rejected not because of racism, but because they lacked the qualifications. Due to prior discrimination, blacks had comparatively less education and experience, which often formed the basis of their rejections. In the arena of residential segregation, the previously all-white suburbs would change little with the ascendance of equality of opportunity, not due to restrictive covenants (or any of the other racist devices described in chapter 2), but because people of color lacked the wealth to relocate there.

These limitations went largely unnoticed in the early years of the civil rights movement, especially when equality of opportunity remained years away (and when its enactment was not yet a foregone conclusion). As James Cone remarks, even such leaders as Malcolm X and Martin Luther King, Jr. initially overlooked these limitations.

> Both men began to analyze the problem of economic injustice during their last years, but the concepts of integration and separation, as they inherited and developed them, did not encourage them to view the American political economy as a primary cause of the oppression of blacks. In fact, it was generally assumed, by both integrationists and separatists, that the American sociopolitical system was basically good and that the *only* thing wrong with it was the exclusion of blacks and other people of color from its benefits.[5]

The collective wisdom, in other words, was that with the inclusion of blacks via equality of opportunity, these other benefits (residential integration, economic equality, and the like) would just sort of "happen." It took more time for them— and the nation at large—to realize that, in the words of Charles W. Mills, "power relations can survive the formal dismantling of their more overt supports."[6] And this is precisely what transpired: the "dismantling" of such power structures as Jim Crow did little to challenge the deeply rooted inequalities that had inundated the nation since its founding. It was possible, in other words, to possess legal racial equality without possessing equality in any other area. Just because racial groups have equal voting rights and the equal opportunity to apply for jobs, it doesn't mean they will also have the same amount of money in their bank accounts or equal access to health care.

Both King and Malcolm X, to be sure, had repudiated their earlier stance by the time the 1964 Civil Rights Act was signed into law. King verbalized his understanding that such equality of opportunity would not produce equality of result with his oft-quoted question, "What good is it to be able to sit at a lunch counter if you can't afford a hamburger?" Here, King echoes my earlier assertions: it is one thing to sit at a previously segregated lunch counter, but completely another to take the next step and actually do something while there (in short, buy a hamburger). As Leon Litwack asserts, equality of opportunity alone "did not provide jobs for the jobless, adequate housing and health care for the poor, or quality integrated education."[7] These turned out to be a different beast entirely: challenges that nonviolent marches could do nothing to overcome.

The same anxieties began circulating among members of the Lyndon Baines Johnson administration. These concerns were summed up succinctly in a report composed by Johnson's assistant secretary of labor (and Harvard sociologist) Daniel Patrick Moynihan. Written in late 1964-early 1965, Moynihan introduced his report by voicing the same concerns that were increasingly engrossing the civil rights movement, opening with the following ominous warning: "The United States is approaching a new crisis in race relations."[8]

The "old crisis"—the crusade for equality of opportunity—had largely been won, and holdovers from the old racist order were fighting a losing battle. As Moynihan declared, "The effort, no matter how savage and brutal, of some State and local governments to thwart the exercise of those rights is doomed. The nation will not put up with it—least of all the Negroes." On these points, Moynihan was absolutely correct, and the nation could set its sights on other matters. "In the meantime," he wrote, "a new period is beginning."[9]

This "new period" revolved around addressing the limitations of equality of opportunity. Employing precisely this language, Moynihan asserted that:

> In this new period the expectations of the Negro Americans will go beyond civil rights. Being Americans, they will now expect that in the near future equal opportunities for them as a group will produce roughly equal results, as compared with other groups. *This is not going to happen.* Nor will it happen for generations to come unless a new and special effort is made.[10]

Here, Moynihan makes clear the administration's own understanding of the limitations of legal racial equality by noting that the expected equality of result would end in disappointment—not simply in the near future, but for "generations to come" if nothing further was done. Moynihan employed a choice of words to describe that next stage—going "beyond civil rights"—that captures the many battles that would envelop the civil rights movement in its later years.

The "Moynihan Report" (as his intervention came to be called) provided a set of specific recommendations for how to move beyond civil rights, and we will assess them in the following section. The themes Moynihan raised took root on the larger stage. Many consider the highwater moment for the government's intention to address the limitations of legal racial equality to be President Johnson's commencement address at Howard University in June 1965. Since Moynihan coauthored his speech, its themes closely parallel the Moynihan Report. Titled "To Fulfill These Rights," Johnson articulated the realization that equality of opportunity, while an important victory, was going to leave most blacks behind. They remained, Johnson put it, "another nation." He continued: "Despite the court orders and the laws, despite the legislative victories and the speeches, for them the walls are rising and the gulf is widening."[11]

Johnson also acknowledged the pattern of residential segregation that had taken hold in the US—the chocolate cities/vanilla suburbs phenomenon: "Moreover, the isolation of Negro from white communities is increasing, rather than decreasing as Negroes crowd into the central cities and become a city within a city."[12] (Importantly, as Ira Katznelson notes, Johnson failed to illuminate the forces responsible for this trend—restrictive covenants, the policies of the Federal Housing Administration, contract leasing, and so forth.)[13]

One of the enduring phrases from Johnson's commencement address was the assertion that "Freedom is not enough." In this, Johnson conceded that at some level, past racism was responsible for creating the racial dilemmas that faced the nation. Equality of opportunity had become the law of the land, which was surely a great achievement—"But freedom is not enough." As Johnson described it, "You do not take a person who, for years, has been hobbled by chains and liberate him, bring him up to the starting line of a race and then say, 'you are free to compete with all the others,' and still justly believe that you have been completely fair."[14] This metaphor of the footrace had much purchase during the mid-1960s; as Eric Sundquist points out, it had been used by both Martin Luther King, Jr. and Daniel Patrick Moynihan for similar ends.[15] In each case, the footrace metaphor was a reference to the "something special" (in King's words) that would need to be done to allow blacks to attain equality of result.

Johnson's follow-up statements turn to the specific issue of equality of opportunity and its inability to produce equality of result. "This is the next and the more profound stage of the battle for civil rights. We seek not just freedom but opportunity. We seek not just legal equity but human ability, not just equality as a right and a theory but equality as a fact and equality as a result."[16] While such iterations were surely radical—especially coming from the white establishment, the government (as will become clear in the next section) had little intention of actually following through and enacting the sweeping legislation required to achieve the "equality as a fact and equality as a result" of which Johnson spoke. His program, Sundquist notes, "was more or less dead on arrival."[17]

Instead, the government busied itself with the task of suppressing the increasing radicalism within many sectors of the civil rights movement. As Moynihan had accurately warned, the "expectations" of blacks would be that "in the near future," equality of opportunity would translate into equality of result. Civil rights groups picked up on Moynihan's realization: that "This [was] not going to happen." Such betrayed expectations triggered a further radicalization of the civil rights movement; whereas nonviolence and the drive toward integration had characterized the movement in its early years, Black Power and other confrontational ideologies took root in the late 1960s. Their demands went well beyond equality of opportunity and involved a thorough racial and economic restructuring of the nation. In addition, several hundred race riots gripped most cities in the US as blacks and others vented their frustrations with poverty, police brutality, and their continued marginalization from the prosperity of the nation. A significant turning point in the civil rights movement occurred in August 1965, when just five days after Johnson signed the Voting Rights Act, the Watts Riots in Los Angeles occurred, which caused thirty-four deaths and over forty million dollars in property damage.

Whatever pledges the government may have made towards seriously addressing the limitations of equality of opportunity had largely vanished by the late 1960s. Instead, they began devoting various energies to subduing the radical factions of the civil rights movement. How they accomplished this—and how it ultimately altered the terrain upon which we think about race and racial inequality—is the topic of the following section.

Suppressing the Radicalism of "Beyond Civil Rights"

The radicalization of the civil rights movement took the nation by storm in the late 1960s. During these tumultuous years, the government faced an ideological and political tug-of-war: on the one hand, they encountered increasing demands to achieve full racial equality of result from such radical civil rights groups as the Black Panthers, to say nothing of dealing with the hundreds of race riots that engulfed the nation's cities. And on the other hand, this increasingly hostile climate had caused many sympathetic whites to withdraw their support for the civil rights movement.

All this placed the government in an awkward position as they attempted to contend with these competing forces. History records that whites (and their palpable resentment for Black Power-type ideologies) would be victorious in this tug-of-war battle. The stated commitments the Johnson administration gave to going "beyond civil rights"—such as in the president's 1965 Howard commencement address—proved to be little more than lip service. In a real sense, they understood the implications of demands for equality of result and the far-reaching and thoroughgoing changes required to make it a reality. But as Howard Winant remarks, the nation never had any intention of making good on the promises they had made to achieve equality between racial groups. "Substantive equality would have meant massive redistribution of resources; it would have clashed with fundamental capitalist class interests; *it was never even on the table*."[18] Winant's parting statement here is important for its reminder that at no point was the government actually considering acquiescing to the demands emanating from a civil rights movement that was becoming more radical and more confrontational at every turn.

Since these demands and riots showed no immediate signs of dissipating, how would the government ultimately restore the racial status quo as painlessly as possible? In dealing with the most radical wings of the civil rights movement, the government accomplished this through a combination of strategies. One tactic involved the overt repression of such groups as the Black Panthers; the FBI's Counter Intelligence Program (COINTELPRO) was tasked with the elimination of these groups, be it through the assassination of key leaders or the implosion of groups from within by fomenting discord and infighting. Such opposition successfully disunified Black Power organizations and blunted their influence. Another strategy involved the granting of limited concessions to radical demands; the establishment of affirmative action programs and Ethnic Studies departments at universities are among the better-known institutional changes. And while these were surely major victories, the government did little more than that.

Suppressing the radicalism of "beyond civil rights" took other forms as well, which make up the main subject of this section. As I wrote at the outset of this chapter, the civil rights movement vastly altered the way we think about race, racism, and racial inequality today. In the midst of the above changes, the very ideas that Americans held concerning racial issues began to shift in unprecedented ways. Investigating several episodes during this moment in history will help us identify these crucial transitions in our thinking about race today. With these transitions, the government successfully quelled the radical elements of the civil rights movement while making only the most minimal institutional changes— the kind that did little to dent the armor of white privilege and push the nation towards true equality of result.

THE MOYNIHAN REPORT AND THE POLITICS OF "BLAMING THE VICTIM"

To begin this investigation, we need to return to the Moynihan Report, discussed briefly in the preceding section. The Johnson administration had asked author Daniel Patrick Moynihan to exercise his skills as a Harvard sociologist to determine why, specifically, equality of opportunity was not going to lead to equality of result. In the Moynihan Report, he attempted to draw their attention to what he considered to be the key problem. To reiterate, Moynihan began his report by acknowledging a fact that was becoming ever more evident to the government and the civil rights movement: that equality of result was going to prove elusive. He also ominously noted that without a "new and special effort," such equality of result would remain generations away. As Moynihan warned, "Indices of dollars of income, standards of living, and years of education deceive. The gap between the Negro and most other groups in American society is widening."

Moynihan then pointed out what he considered to be the source of this conundrum: and its solution:

The fundamental problem, in which this is most clearly the case, is that of family structure. The evidence—not final, but powerfully persuasive—is that the Negro family in the urban ghettos is crumbling. A middle class group has managed to save itself, but for vast numbers of the unskilled, poorly educated city working class the fabric of conventional social relationships has all but disintegrated. There are indications that the situation may have been arrested in the past few years, but the general post war trend is unmistakable. So long as this situation persists, the cycle of poverty and disadvantage will continue to repeat itself.[19]

In sum, Moynihan's central argument was that the disintegration of the black family would be the reason they would fail to achieve equality of result. Much of his report painted a grim portrait of the black family, from their reliance on government assistance to the percentage of female-headed households to the epidemic of out-of-wedlock births. More tellingly (and controversially), Moynihan's point of view was that these forces were self-perpetuating. As Moynihan described it, the crumbling black family had initiated a "cycle of poverty and disadvantage" that would "continue to repeat itself" with or without white racism, equality of opportunity, or any other racial factor. It had assumed a life of its own, independent of whatever forces had been responsible for its creation.

The Moynihan Report (whose official title was "The Negro Family: The Case for National Action") was an internal document not meant for public consumption. While the report was published in March 1965, the debate truly began that summer, when the report was leaked to the press and became public. The Moynihan Report elicited polarizing reactions, gaining the adoration of some and the contempt of others.

Many individuals praised the Moynihan Report because it took the responsibility off whites for the persistence of racial inequality. In other words, the implication was that if blacks wanted to attain equality of result, *they* would be the ones that would need to change. Under this reading, the persistence of black poverty had nothing to do with the impact of centuries of white racism; rather, blacks would remain poor and disadvantaged due to their own shortcomings as a race (specifically, in the mismanagement of their families). As Leon Litwack notes, the idea that it was blacks' own fault that they would remain poor "had obvious appeal," because it suggested that whites were in no way implicated in their plight. "If it's their fault," the saying went, "then *we* don't have to do anything."[20]

Others, however, were outraged by Moynihan's conclusions. They argued, in contrast, that the condition of the black family had everything to do with slavery, Jim Crow, and the myriad other ways whites had ravaged blacks for their own material gain. While such critics neither disputed Moynihan's data nor denied the precarious condition of the black family, they contended that he had confused cause and effect. The Moynihan Report had suggested that the crumbling black family was the *cause* of their continued poverty and inability to obtain equality of result. Moynihan's detractors viewed it the other way around, insisting that the collapsing black family was the *effect* of poverty and racism.

Placing himself at the forefront of these criticisms of the Moynihan Report was Boston psychologist William Ryan, who accused Moynihan of "blaming the victim." Despite the fact that blacks had been victimized at the hands of white racism, Moynihan was ultimately blaming them for their failures, when in Ryan's view, the responsibility should be placed squarely at the doorstep of antiblack policies. The concept of blaming the victim became the primary phrase by which critics came to articulate their profound reservations with Moynihan's conclusions and all that they implied.

Ryan wrote a book (itself titled *Blaming the Victim*) in 1970, which expounded upon the themes he had originally formulated in opposition to the Moynihan Report. As Ryan remarks, "Pointing to the supposedly deviant Negro family as the 'fundamental weakness of the Negro community' is [one] way to blame the victim." Ryan assaulted the belief systems of those convinced that "Growing up in the 'crumbling' Negro family is supposed to account for most of the racial evils in America." With a touch of sarcasm, he retorts, "Is it any wonder the Negroes cannot achieve equality? From such families!"[21]

For Ryan, blaming the victim carries with it consequences guaranteed to obstruct the path to racial justice. "...[B]y focusing our attention on the Negro family as the apparent *cause* of racial inequality," Ryan asserts, "our eye is diverted. Racism, discrimination, segregation, and the powerlessness of the ghetto are subtly, but thoroughly, downgraded in importance."[22] Key to this crucial passage is the confusion the Moynihan Report made between cause and effect that I related earlier; by placing an obsessive amount of attention on the breakdown of the black family, the forces responsible for that breakdown fade safely into the background. We analyzed many of those forces in chapter 2: the policies of the New Deal as well as the Federal Housing Administration, which channeled resources away from these same black families and towards whites who were rapidly relocating to resource-rich vanilla suburbs. In the view of Ryan and many others, these developments should take center stage in assessing the racial situation of the black family. In contrast, for white conservatives and others interested in maintaining the racial status quo, blaming the victim proved enormously cost-effective, essentially deleting the impact of these same forces and allowing whites to keep hold of the advantages they had accrued from them. In such an environment, there would be no reason to pursue equality of result, since it was blacks who had shot themselves in the foot.

CONTRACT LEASING: AN EARLY INSTANCE OF "BLAMING THE VICTIM"

The concept of blaming the victim, to be sure, predates the Moynihan Report and the brouhaha that ensued. The tendency to only look at the destructive effects of racism emerges in a variety of forms and places. One powerful instance of blaming the victim materializes in the practice of contract leasing, which we first explored in chapter 2.

To recall, contract leasing involved the exploitation of blacks at the hands of the Federal Housing Administration and white real estate speculators. Since the FHA had redlined black neighborhoods, there was no way for the overwhelming majority of black families to purchase their own homes. In addition, blacks could not buy homes in the suburbs because restrictive covenants and similar mechanisms effectively barred their entry. White speculators capitalized on this situation, buying properties in black redlined neighborhoods and leasing them on contract to blacks at excessively inflated prices. As discussed in chapter 2, such deals led to countless prospective homebuyers missing payments and ultimately getting evicted from their homes.

If such mass evictions occurred, it wasn't because blacks didn't make the effort to keep up with their payments. They used several methods. For instance, they would subdivide the home and bring in extra people so that they could contribute their added incomes toward paying their contract seller (this had the effect of increasing population density, with all the consequences that accompany it). Many families worked longer hours or took on another job in an attempt to keep up with the terms of the contract lease (this had the effect of leaving children more unsupervised). Their attempts to keep from losing their homes to the contract sellers caused these and other negative outcomes, which produced a notable downturn in the quality of black communities affected by contract leasing. Most whites, however, did not see the exploitation at the heart of this downturn; as Beryl Satter writes:

> The resulting decline of racially changing areas fed white racism. If black contract buyers saw themselves making heroic sacrifices against impossible odds to keep from falling behind on their payments, this was not how their white neighbors viewed the situation. Whites saw population densities doubling, while garbage collection and other municipal services stayed the same or declined. They saw unsupervised children flooding the neighborhood. They noted that buildings bought by African Americans rapidly decayed. Small wonder that whites blamed their black neighbors for the chaos they observed.[23]

The situation of contract leasing (and the blaming of the victim that ensued) teaches us important lessons about racism. When most whites viewed black neighborhoods beset by the scourge of contract leasing, they only saw the end result: the filth in the area, the unsupervised children milling about, and so forth. They neglected to acknowledge the root of the issue: the exploitation of contract leasing. William Ryan and those sharing his criticisms of the Moynihan Report highlighted the same point, namely, the refusal to target the background of what was causing black families to fall apart as central to uncovering its solution.

The consequences of contract leasing likewise demonstrate the ways racism becomes *justified*. As Satter noted above, since whites only saw the destructive effects of contract leasing (rather than the exploitation at its core), it came as little surprise that they blamed blacks themselves for the deterioration of their communities. This became the basis of how whites justified keeping blacks out of their own neighborhoods through such devices as restrictive covenants. If areas occupied by blacks declined, so the reasoning went, it made perfect sense to keep them out of white locales, as their entry would negatively impact the area's property values. All this, of course, represents the racism merry-go-round, as it was the very practice of excluding blacks that exposed them to contract leasing in the first place. Contract leasing's destructive effects then allowed whites to feel justified in continuing to bar blacks from their communities.

This obsessive determination to keep suburban neighborhoods all-white extended into the 1970s—years after equality of opportunity had become the law of the land. In his book, *Colored Property*, historian David Freund shares the story of one Giuseppe Stanzione, a white man living in the all-white suburb of Dearborn, just outside of Detroit. In September 1963, an angry white mob confronted him at his home because they had learned he had sold it to a black family. This mob (which consisted of several hundred residents of the area) threw bottles and stones at his home, and they slashed the tires of his car and poured sugar in the fuel tank. The mob only dispersed upon learning that Stanzione had rented the home to a white family—who had in turn hired blacks to move in their belongings.[24]

The Stanzione episode exemplifies the determination of whites to keep blacks out of their suburban neighborhoods. Several points stand out. The first, as Freund remarks, is that the white mob would have never considered their actions to have been "racist": they were simply protecting the purity of their neighborhood and the value of their property from blacks whose presence would surely damage both (thus the origin of the saying, "There goes the neighborhood."). But it again blurs the larger context; if areas where blacks lived declined, its root was not black behavior, but white racism in such forms as contract leasing. Since that context was removed, it allowed whites to feel fully justified in taking whatever actions necessary to keep their neighborhoods white—up to and including mob violence.

In both the catastrophic consequences of contract leasing as well as the crumbling black family, the background to black behavior is ignored and dismissed. We can consider this issue from the other side: if white families were relatively stable, could it be in part the product of their living in safe communities with great resources and access to well-paying jobs? Whatever the case may be, the ideology of blaming the victim prevents us from even asking those sorts of questions. As William Ryan points out, since the tendency is to only look at the victim, "The formula for action becomes extraordinarily simple: change the victim," rather than the circumstances that have produced the victim.[25]

In the end, blaming the victim became one of the primary ways the government successfully sidestepped the prospect of making the substantive institutional changes required to obtain equality of result. Blaming blacks for their own shortcomings provided an ideal outlet for those looking to suppress the civil rights revolution in ways that did not parallel too closely the murderous tactics the Soviets used to keep their communist society in order. And indeed, by placing the responsibility upon blacks themselves, they end up not looking like "victims" at all, but rather a people who have dug their own graves and thus deserve their unequal status.

THE MODEL MINORITY MYTH

The tendency to blame blacks and other groups of color for their own poverty and deprivation persists in the 21st Century; it remains one of the primary ways to silence continued efforts to attain material racial equality in US society. It represents a way of thinking that we have inherited from the racial turbulence of the civil rights movement, and for many Americans, it nixes whatever sympathy they might otherwise hold for the enduring degradation and poverty that continues to consume our nation's inner cities.

This way of thinking became reinforced less than a year after the Moynihan Report first introduced and popularized it. In January 1966, sociologist William Petersen published an article in *Newsweek* magazine entitled "Success Story Japanese-American Style." Petersen extolled Japanese Americans for their apparent success in the US in the face of such racism as their forced relegation in internment camps during World War II. In December of the same year, another article appeared in *U.S. News & World Report*, bearing the title, "Success Story of One Minority in the U.S." In this case, Chinese Americans fell under the flattering spotlight in ways that closely paralleled the praises Petersen had placed upon Japanese Americans.

These two articles signaled the ascendance of what soon came to be labeled the "model minority myth." As I have elsewhere defined it, the model minority myth is "the culturally-driven ideology that Asian Americans have achieved success in US society in spite of the race-related obstacles they have faced."[26] Both Petersen and the author(s) of the *U.S. News & World Report* article sought to showcase the success of Asian Americans and their ability to claim hold of the American Dream no matter the obstacle. They provided data that suggested that Asian Americans' household income was closely on par with that of whites.

Early critics of the model minority myth exposed the flawed data of these income comparisons, demonstrating that Asian Americans hadn't achieved the level of success that its inventors had insinuated. For one, they didn't take into account the fact that Asian Americans were more likely than whites to live in urban areas (comparing only whites and Asian Americans from urban areas revealed a fissure between their income levels). Furthermore, the inventors of the myth failed to note that Asian Americans had, on average, more workers per household—if they had compared *individual* incomes (rather than household incomes), the gap between the two groups would have been shown to be much wider.

Of course, data accuracy was not the primary objective; the model minority myth was at bottom a *calculated political maneuver* designed to silence the radical elements of the civil rights movement who were demanding systemic changes to the very framework of society. The whole point was to compare blacks to another nonwhite racial group—Asian Americans—who had apparently experienced "success" in American society. Indeed, this comparison is embedded in the term itself, "*model* minority myth"—model for who? A model for other groups of color who, instead of getting their own lives (and families) in order, spent their time crying "racism" and expecting the government to provide them free handouts (and rioting when the latter didn't occur).

That the independent desire to uplift Asian Americans was not the true goal of those who invented the model minority myth was made plain by the author(s) of the *U.S. News & World Report* article: "At a time when it is being proposed that hundreds of billions be spent to uplift Negroes and other minorities, the nation's 300,000 Chinese Americans are moving ahead on their own, with no help from anyone else."[27] Here, the connection between the radical demands of the civil rights movement and the praising of Asian Americans becomes evident—and their real agenda emerges. While blacks "and other minorities" were making excessive demands on the government, Chinese Americans were realizing the American Dream "with no help from anyone else." The ultimate purpose of the model minority myth was to say (in particular) to blacks, "If you were like Asian

Americans, you would be successful too." This comparison was particularly valuable because the group receiving the praise had, like blacks, a history of being on the business end of racial discrimination.

Likewise important was not simply the ostensible fact of Asian American success, but *why* they had experienced such success. In this case, the belief was that Asian Americans had a strong value system that contributed to their ability to overcome obstacles: precisely what the Moynihan Report had implied that blacks lacked. The myth communicated the message that, rather than insisting that "hundreds of billions" be spent on their needs, blacks should adopt the value system that the myth's inventors believed lay at the heart of Asian American success.

The model minority myth continues to resonate strongly today; along with the notion that Asian Americans are "forever foreigners," the myth remains among the most powerful stereotypes afflicting Asian Americans. Today, the myth is buttressed not by income comparisons (as was the case at the moment of its 1966 invention), but rather their success in education. In this case, Asian American educational achievements are uncontested—they outperform other racial groups (including whites) to a significant degree. As before, the question becomes *why* their accomplishments in education prove so outstanding. The model minority-prompted rationale again focuses on their value system: in a word, Asian Americans' appreciation for education that logically leads to their success.

Missing from this account is the 1965 Immigration Act, one of the main pieces of legislation passed in response to the civil rights movement. Prior to this act, Asians had been all but fully excluded from immigrating to the country for decades; the 1965 Immigration Act provided a quota of 20,000 immigrants per year per country, which prompted a massive increase in the number of Asians immigrating to the US (indeed, roughly two-thirds of Asian Americans today can trace their immigrant heritage to this Immigration Act). It vastly shaped the demographics of Asian America.

The 1965 Immigration Act, however, was very selective; it contained a variety of filters that affected the likelihood of whether a given individual would be granted entry to the US. For example, the act gave preference to prospective immigrants who had family members already residing in the US, and in a stab at the Soviet Union, it provided generous allotments to political refugees. Lastly—and most important for our purposes here—the Immigration Act contained a "preference to professionals" clause, which meant that people who already possessed advanced degrees and high-skilled jobs would have a greater chance of entering the US. Immigration data shows that Asian took by far the most advantage of the preference to professionals clause, making them "a very biased sample, the cream of their own societies."[28] So while Asian Americans have surely achieved high marks in education, it is necessary to keep in mind that they were, in the words of Stephen Steinberg, "'successful' even before their arrival in America."[29]

The effect of the 1965 Immigration Act upon the educational prospects of Asian Americans becomes clear when we ascertain when they started attending universities at rates far above their percentage of the population. As Timothy Fong notes, the spike in Asian American enrollment occurred in the late 1970s and early 1980s—just as the children of these immigrants entering through the preference to professionals clause of the Immigration Act were starting to reach college age.[30] (The main predictor of whether a child will go to college remains whether his or her parents attended college.)

With the model minority myth, we see the same mentality at work that we did with the Moynihan Report and contract leasing. In each case, the background to success or failure becomes deleted, be it white exploitation or selective immigration policy. All we see is the end results: degraded neighborhoods, broken families—or in the case of Asian Americans, smashing success. In the context of the late 1960s and the demands for the government to create true equality of result, the common denominator between the Moynihan Report and the model minority myth was the same: they both functioned as ideological devices designed to suppress and silence those demands and restore the racial status quo.

RETHINKING THE "WHY" OF RACIAL INEQUALITY

Collectively, the Moynihan Report and the model minority myth did more than help the nation move beyond the civil rights movement without having to significantly redistribute resources away from whites and towards communities of color. Whether intentionally or not, they became the catalysts for altering the way Americans conceive of racial inequality—more specifically, they ushered in the rise to dominance of a new way of thinking about "why" racial inequality exists in our society.

For approximately a century prior to the civil rights movement, the predominant justification given for racial inequality can be placed under the label "Social Darwinism." In this "survival of the fittest" world, whites had attained racial hegemony due to their superior biological makeup. In other words, the root of white domination lay in biology; if whites controlled most of the world (which they did at the beginning of the 20th Century), it was because of their superior intelligence and other genetically-based attributes. One influential strand of this ideology was known as "eugenics," which was the basis of Hitler's anti-Semitism and his Final Solution to exterminate Jews.

Owing to the Holocaust and other significant world developments (such as the anticolonial movements described earlier in this chapter), Social Darwinism began to fall out of favor just as the civil rights movement was picking up steam in the US. In this change of perspective, biology would no longer dominate in explaining why certain racial groups succeed and others fail. At issue becomes the following: as this chapter has illuminated, racial inequality would persist in a post-Social Darwinist era. Despite the implementation of equality of opportunity, the educational and economic performance of racial groups would continue to differ sharply. With Social Darwinism discredited and out of the picture, how would persisting racial inequality be justified in an equal opportunity world?

The justification that ultimately emerged ended up looking quite a bit like the Social Darwinism that had been left behind. As Stephen Steinberg notes, in spite of all the changes the civil rights movement produced, "modern social science has not transcended the logic and values of Social Darwinism as completely as is generally supposed. All too often, notions of biological superiority and inferiority have been replaced with a new set of ideas that amount to claims of *cultural* superiority and inferiority."[31] And the vehicles for this replacement from biology to culture were the Moynihan Report and the model minority myth.

Our examination above of the Moynihan Report and the model minority showcase this difference. According to the former, blacks would continue to languish at the margins of society because they possessed the wrong culture in the form of broken families, overreliance on welfare, and so forth. The model minority myth made the same point, but from the opposite angle: Asian Americans were successful because they possessed the right culture in the form of an appreciation for education and family values. While the details between the two differed, *they were communicating the exact same message*: that success befalls those with the "right" values, while groups that have the "wrong" values are doomed to fail. And they were both political maneuvers designed to silence groups that continued to make demands on the government for racial equality of result.

Thus, with the Moynihan Report and the model minority myth, a new way of justifying racial inequality came to the fore, a concept Stephen Steinberg calls the "cultural survival of the fittest" ideology. As Steinberg defines it, with this ideology, "The principle of the survival of the fittest still holds, though it is now defined in cultural rather than biological terms."[32] The root of racial group success and failure no longer has its basis in biology, but in culture and values. In their article, "Are Blacks Color Blind Too?," Eduardo Bonilla-Silva and David G. Embrick term this same concept the "biologization of culture," because culture is interpreted as being just as much a part of one's heredity as biology.[33] To quote Steinberg again on this point, "culture is inherited just as inexorably as if it had been implanted in the genes."[34]

Whether in its Social Darwinist or "cultural survival of the fittest" version, the end result is the same: the rationalization of continued racial inequality. This is how the US would now justify white privilege in a society where opportunities are equal and racial discrimination has been rendered illegal: "*they* just don't work hard enough, and *they* don't take advantage of the opportunities coming their way." Since the legal obstacles to racial equality have now been removed, if blacks and other groups of color still cannot "make it" in society, they have no one to blame but themselves.

Conclusion: "A Victim of its Own Success"

In 1967, Lee Rainwater and William Yancey made the following prediction: "The year 1965 may be known in history as the time when the civil rights movement discovered, in the sense of becoming explicitly aware, that abolishing legal racism would not produce Negro equality."[35] Time, of course, has proven them correct: just as the different pieces of civil rights legislation were being successfully pushed through Congress, the various sectors of society—from the government to civil rights groups—became "explicitly aware" that the implementation of equality of opportunity was not going to produce anything even distantly resembling equality of result. Essentially every racial battle that occurred during the late 1960s can trace its source back to this realization; it was the centerpiece that animated the struggles and counterstruggles that consumed the nation during these frenzied and chaotic years.

As radical civil rights groups fought and rioted to make equality of result a reality, the government made every effort to stem the conflagration. While they used blatant shows of force (such as with COINTELPRO), they made a more wide-ranging impact on the ideological arena: with the Moynihan Report and the model minority myth, the persistence of white privilege and nonwhite deprivation could now be traced to culture and values, rather than to the legacy of slavery and Jim Crow. Blaming the victim in this way becomes, as William Ryan put it, "an ideal, almost painless evasion,"[36] since the fault for continued racial inequality gets placed upon those groups that remain at the bottom of society. And in that blame, all the privileges that whites would continue to possess—such as the wealth they had acquired during their FHA-prompted exodus to the wealthy suburbs—drop out of the discussion.

The civil rights movement remains a landmark in American history. No one can question the intrepidity of those early civil rights marchers, who braved the fury of the white racist establishment so that all Americans, regardless of race, could have the same opportunity to vote, to sit at a lunch counter, or to live wherever they desired. Martin Luther King, Jr. rightly inspired the nation (and beyond) with his speech, "I Have a Dream." All this, however, came to expose how deeply rooted race and racism were in the very fabric of the nation, as the victories of the civil rights movement produced the realization that equality of opportunity alone would do little to upset the institutional pattern of white privilege and nonwhite disadvantage. The battles of the late 1960s broadcast the profound limitations of the early civil rights vision—a time in which radical groups forced the issue among the government by demanding changes in the very framework of society. The government's response, this chapter has illuminated, was to silence those demands using whatever methods lay at their disposal.

In retrospective commentaries of this period, it is common for analysts to claim that the civil rights movement was "a victim of its own success." Essentially all the objectives of the early civil rights agenda were realized: antidiscrimination legislation, voting rights, immigration reform, and so forth. Yet in the aura of all these victories, writes Harvard Sitkoff, "the movement created aspirations it could not fulfill,"[37] with the government ensuring that most of those aspirations would remain frustrated. And for many supportive whites, the battle had been won upon the passage of the above civil rights legislation; with Jim Crow entering its own grave, what more needed to be accomplished? It was little wonder, then, that many of them ceased supporting the civil rights movement as the level and intensity of the demands for equality of result increased. In the same way, the government began turning its back on racial justice and sought to maintain the racial status quo by introducing the most minimal changes possible.

By the mid-1970s, the modern civil rights movement had all but come to an end, bringing the nation to our current moment, the post-civil rights era. Scrutinized as a whole, the civil rights movement ushered in a great number of positive changes to the US. But it also possessed an equal number of shortcomings, which did little to create true justice for all racial groups. Douglas Massey soberly communicates the dismal reality that the civil rights movement left behind: "not only did the civil rights legislation of the 1960s and 1970s fail to end racial stratification in the United States, but in some ways it gave birth even more pernicious and intractable mechanisms of categorical inequality."[38] For example, by not eliminating racial wealth inequality, whites would still possess a powerful mechanism by which to hold on to their privileges and pass them along to the next generation. As chapter 1 related, it did not require the presence of "racist" people (whom the civil rights movement marginalized) or Jim Crow-type systems (which the movement vanquished) for whites to retain advantages in the area of wealth. And with the switch from Social Darwinism to "cultural survival of the fittest" rhetoric, defenders of the racial status quo now possess a formidable ideological mechanism by which to deflect continuing demands to eliminate the various racial inequalities that the civil rights movement proved unable to touch. These battles for racial justice are still being fought today.

Questions

What had you learned about the civil rights movement prior to reading this chapter? How has our discussion here altered your views of the movement?

As the early civil rights movement pursued legal racial equality, why do you think they initially missed the realization that equality of opportunity was not going to lead to equality of result?

In what other ways do we see "blaming the victim" occur in our society?

Recalling our analysis of contrast leasing in this chapter, why do you think people tend to focus on the *effects* of racism (broken families, deteriorating neighborhoods, etc.) rather than its roots? In the same way, why do you think people often focus exclusively on Asian American "culture" as the reason for their supposed "success," rather than looking at immigration policies that encouraged the already successful to immigrate here in significant numbers?

Why have we yet to see another civil rights movement, one that tackles racial inequality in all its forms?

Chapter 4

The Hysterics of Affirmative Action

Introduction

About a decade ago, the University of Texas system adopted an admissions policy known as the "Ten Percent Plan." Under this policy, which covers all public schools in Texas, high school students who graduate in the top 10% of their particular school would be guaranteed admission to the University of Texas. The Ten Percent Plan had the purpose of introducing a greater degree of racial and class diversity at the university by attempting to create a more level playing field. Since many high schools (especially in the inner cities) are comparatively underfunded and have less access to (for example) honors classes and SAT prep courses, students attending them become artificially disadvantaged. The Ten Percent Plan was designed to counteract those disadvantages and give all high school students an equal shot at entering the University of Texas.

The Ten Percent Plan, however, only fills about 80% of the freshmen slots. To fill the remaining seats, the University of Texas employed racial "affirmative action," in which race would be used as one factor among many in selecting the remaining high school students who would make up the freshmen class at the university. Like the Ten Percent Plan, affirmative action functioned as a tool to ramp up racial diversity in the college population.

Abigail Fisher applied to the University of Texas at Austin in 2008. She could not be admitted through the Ten Percent Plan, as she missed the cutoff, graduating instead in the top 12% of her high school senior class. Her application became part of the pool of remaining slots—those spaces in which affirmative action would factor into the admissions process. After the University of Texas rejected her, she sued the university system, claiming that she had been discriminated against because she is white. In October 2012, the Supreme Court heard oral arguments in *Fisher v. Texas*, and as of this writing, the Justices have yet to reach a verdict.

Whatever their judgment, the saga of Abigail Fisher has placed affirmative action back at the epicenter of the racial disputes that envelop this nation. Affirmative action remains among the most contentious programs in existence, winning the adulation of some and the consternation of many others. Because of this, affirmative action grants an ideal point of entry into many of the doubts and fears that surround the concept of racism itself. This chapter wades into this prickly debate, providing an introductory excavation into its history and purpose. Analyzing the positions of those who love—and those who loathe—the program will communicate a great deal about where we stand as a nation regarding racial matters today.

To its proponents, affirmative action is a necessary tool that redresses the legacy of racial oppression in our society by seeking to include previously excluded groups. As chapter 3 briefly detailed, affirmative action became the most significant program that went into wide-scale operation with the intention of achieving "equality of result." Whites would remain racially privileged, such supporters reasoned, necessitating the presence of a program that could act as a way to counterbalance those privileges.

To its opponents, affirmative action compromises the integrity of hiring and admissions policies by introducing factors—in this case, race and gender—which are viewed as unrelated to performance and thus providing an unfair advantage to certain groups "just because" they happen to be members of those groups. To its naysayers, affirmative action offends the cherished American values of individualism and merit; it bestows undeserved advantages to college and job applicants on the basis of attributes that they believe should be ignored.

This chapter overviews some of the critical debates surrounding affirmative action, a policy conceived in the context of the realization that equality of opportunity would not seamlessly translate into racial equality of result. As the first section will relate, I'm not primarily interested in describing in detail the specific forms affirmative action has taken; rather, I place my focus on its *principle*, that is, the actual purpose behind the program. Later sections delve into the various points of opposition to affirmative action, such as the belief that it constitutes "reverse discrimination" against whites because of the way it gives preferences to people of color. It is those racial preferences, of course, that constitute the source of the contempt that many express towards affirmative action, as its detractors find such preferences anathema and an offense to fairness and objectivity. What our foray into the affirmative action debate will allow us to do is to take the concept of "preference" itself and place it under the microscope. As we shall see, preferences abound in our nation, and while few of these preferences are directly racial in nature, they serve to benefit whites more often than people of color. I closely inquire why the specifically *racial* preferences embedded in affirmative action become the object of such scrutiny in contrast to the countless other preferences that function alongside it.

In chapter 1, I pointed out why I spend an extended amount of time examining affirmative action. Whether I appear to favor the program or not becomes secondary to what a discussion of it can enable. The legacy left behind by pre-civil rights racial oppression forces a confrontation between those who wish to redress that legacy and those who wish to maintain the racial status quo. For better or worse, the very existence of affirmative action programs compels us to acknowledge the presence of racial inequality. It requires that we ask: Why does racial inequality even exist in the first place? Should anything be done about it at all? If so, what can (and should) we do to eliminate it from society? And, lastly, is affirmative action the most effective way to confront and eradicate racial inequality? Whatever our replies to these inquiries, the spectrum of emotions affirmative action evokes is a strong indication of the many nerves race still manages to touch, as the reactions enveloping *Fisher v. Texas* make evident. Diving headfirst into the affirmative action debate will allow us to see why.

The Principle of Affirmative Action

Over the course of its relatively brief history, affirmative action has taken on a variety of forms. This makes defining the practice of affirmative action difficult, since most universities and companies that employ the program in their admissions and hiring policies do so in different ways. The affirmative action program at the heart of *Fisher v. Texas* is just one manifestation—and one that is unique, as no other university employs affirmative action in quite the same way. Shorn of its specifics, the common thread of all affirmative action programs is the promotion of racial preferences in hiring for jobs and admissions to universities (affirmative action is also gender-based, though our focus will be on its racial manifestations). Again, the actual operation of those preferences differs (often sharply) from place to place, making an extended analysis of the practices of affirmative action cumbersome and unwieldy.

To arrive at a deeper understanding of affirmative action, then, we need to step away from these various "practices" and focus instead on the *principle* of affirmative action. Upon its creation in the civil rights movement, what was affirmative action ultimately attempting to accomplish? We can define its principle in the following way: A *means to neutralize the present-day effects of past racial discrimination*. This principle echoes one of the main points we've encountered in previous chapters—specifically, the position held by many that the *legacy* of pre-civil rights racial discrimination remains with us today in a variety of forms. And if slavery, Jim Crow, and other manifestations of legal racism have produced present-day effects, the purpose of affirmative action was to neutralize those effects and create a level playing field upon which all racial groups could fairly compete.

Let's look at some specific expressions of "the present-day effects" of the racial discrimination that occurred in the past. The practice of "seniority" represents one such example. One gains seniority in a workplace, of course, through years of employment; with such seniority comes such perquisites as higher pay, job security, and so forth. In the abstract, seniority is a perfectly morally defensible practice that rewards one's commitment and dedication to a company. Furthermore, seniority is not in itself a "racial" phenomenon—nor was it designed as a scheme to disadvantage people of color.[1]

How, then, does seniority become a notable example of a present-day effect of past racial discrimination? In the 1970s—about a decade after the implementation of affirmative action—the United States faced its worst economic crisis since the Great Depression (recently supplanted by the Great Recession which began in 2008). In this crisis of what came to be known as "stagflation,"

1. Seniority
2. old boy's networks
3. the legacy clause.

unemployment increased as many businesses began laying off workers due to downsizing, bankruptcy, or relocating overseas in search of cheaper labor. In this instance, blacks were more likely than whites to lose their jobs—not because they were black, but because they lacked seniority. (Some were fired due to racism, of course.) And the reason they lacked seniority is because many of them had just started working for businesses that had been discriminating against them prior to the passage of the 1964 Civil Rights Act.

Seniority thus represents a key instance of how racial discrimination in the past has produced racial effects in the present. As pointed out above, seniority is in the abstract unrelated to race. But when placed in the context of racism in US history, seniority *becomes* racial, since whites have, on average, higher levels of seniority than their nonwhite counterparts. Despite the disappearance of legal racism in the form of "No Blacks Need Apply" signs, blacks would remain disadvantaged due to the lack of seniority they had inherited as a result of that legal racism.

All this bleeds into another example of the present-day effects of past racial discrimination: a concept popularly known as "old boys' networks." It is commonly estimated that approximately 80% of jobs are secured by word-of-mouth connections, rather than through informal job listings in the classified ads or elsewhere. (As the saying goes, it's not "what you know," but "*who* you know.") Philosopher Lawrence Blum discusses both the logic behind old boys' networks as well as the racial impacts they deliver. Such networking, Blum writes:

> saves publicity costs, and it garners job applicants for whom a reliable worker has vouched, thus saving on the costs of assessing job suitability in a larger group of unknown applicants. Nevertheless, such recruiting has a disparate racial impact similar to that of seniority; in many occupations blacks and Latinos constitute a smaller proportion of the workforce than their percentage in the population, and workers' networks are generally race-specific. Thus word-of-mouth recruiting perpetuates racial injustice and sustains the legacy of racial discrimination.[2]

As a result of racial discrimination in previous eras, old boys' networks have been fashioned in such a way that whites have greater access to them.

A final example of the present-day effects of past racial discrimination is the "legacy clause": the preference given to children of alumni at selective universities. Often derided as "affirmative action for the wealthy" by its critics, the legacy clause ensures that certain individuals will have a much greater chance of securing admission to an elite university because at least one parent graduated from that same university. In January 2003, for example, *The Wall Street Journal* reported that Harvard accepts 40% of applicants who are the children of alumni, as opposed to 11% of applicants generally. Similar statistics hold true of other elite universities, both inside and outside the Ivy League.[3] As with seniority and old boys' networks, the legacy clause possesses a rationale of its own: admitting generations of family members increases the likelihood that they will donate money to the university. The legacy clause also parallels seniority and old boys' networks in another way: while the legacy clause is not itself "racial," it has a racial effect since whites disproportionately benefit from it. Due to the racial discrimination of the past, elite universities were almost exclusively white until the civil rights movement; and as a result, people of color are less likely to have parents who attended universities that employ the legacy clause. Like seniority and old boys' networks, the legacy clause operates as a racial privilege in the context of historical racial oppression.

We could expand this list many times over. In seniority, old boys' networks, and the legacy clause, we witness just some of the ways whites continue to carry advantages with them in an era of equality of opportunity. Those advantages were forged in the cauldron of the de jure racism that governed the ages of slavery and Jim Crow and passed down via seniority, wealth inheritance, and myriad other forms—a time "when affirmative action was white," in Ira Katznelson's cunning reference to the New Deal policies examined in chapter 2. And, as we discussed in chapter 1, whites will reap these advantages whether they are "racist" or not. On the other side of the racial divide, people of color confront the underside of the consequences of this de jure racism. Charles W. Mills illuminates this debate further; as he writes, because of racism in the past, people of color today:

> bring to the table a thinner package of assets than they otherwise would have had, and so they will be in a weaker bargaining position than they otherwise would have been. Whites are differentially benefited by this history insofar as they have a competitive advantage that is not the result, or not completely the result, of innate ability and effort but rather of the legacy they have inherited. So unfairness here is manifest

in the failure to redress this legacy, which makes the perpetuation of domination the most likely outcome.[4]

Whatever praises or criticisms we may hold over affirmative action in practice, *this was what affirmative action was designed for in principle:* a way of redressing the legacy of past racism and how its effects continue to plague society's efforts toward racial reconciliation.

Yet affirmative action's plethora of opponents persistently peg the program as unmeritorious, alleging that it unfairly burdens whites. Whether or not affirmative action policies actually "do" burden whites, our discussion in this section has demonstrated how other preference systems burden people of color in similar ways (and thus affirmative action was deemed necessary as a tool to *neutralize* that burden). The question becomes: Why are the racial preferences of affirmative action the object of such scrutiny, while these other preferences slide by relatively undisturbed, despite the benefits they confer to whites? It is to a discussion of this question that I now turn.

To Be or Not to Be...Racial

The examples of seniority, old boys' networks, and the legacy clause teach us exactly how pervasive "preference" is in US society. Americans' unease regarding such preference systems, however, do not approach the contempt many feel toward the racial preferences embedded in affirmative action. This was one of the central dilemmas that journalist Ellis Cose encountered in his book, *The Rage of a Privileged Class.* Speaking about objectively nonracial preferences in general (and the legacy clause in particular), Cose wonders why "nonracial preferences never seem to elicit anything like the animosity provoked by so-called racial quotas."[5] Affirmative action's opponents consistently accuse it as unfairly benefitting "unqualified" applicants, but as Cose notes, "If that were the only issue, programs favoring the children of alumni, say, would provoke the same animus directed at affirmative action."[6] In these two statements, Cose makes an important point about some of the contradictions that swirl around the use of preferences in college admissions and hiring for jobs. As I pointed out in the previous section, people reserve their opprobrium for racial preferences, while other forms of preference pass by relatively unscathed, such as the legacy clause, which Cose highlights here. To put this another way: There's something about *racial* preferences that bother us in a way that nonracial preferences don't. As a racial preference, then, affirmative action has a target placed on it that these other forms of preference do not possess.

It is here that we encounter one of the key dilemmas enveloping affirmative action specifically and racial justice more generally. Seniority, old boys' networks, and the legacy clause may be (on the surface) nonracial preferences—but they all produce racial effects in the context of past racial discrimination. So, in an important sense, they *become* racial preferences, though they are not seen as such by most members of US society. To repeat: affirmative action's initial purpose was to *neutralize* the advantages whites were still receiving from these other ostensibly nonracial privileges (we could add racial wealth inequality to this list). But since these preferences are not technically racial, many do not see them as racial at all, and thus do not acknowledge the benefits whites receive from them.

Part of the challenge, of course, stems from the fact that such preferences as seniority are not directly racial. To return to the example of the layoffs occurring amidst the stagflation crisis of the 1970s, seniority assured that whites were more likely to keep their jobs. However, this protection wasn't absolute; in that decade, some whites lost their jobs because they lacked seniority—and some blacks kept their jobs because they *did* have seniority. A similar pattern emerges with the legacy clause, as few whites have parents who attended universities which give preference to the children of alumni (and, to add another layer of complexity to this subject, it should be noted that another racial group is increasingly reaping the privileges of the legacy clause: Asian Americans).

This is not the case for affirmative action, a program that places its racial preferences front and center; forming its very lifeblood, racial preferences are indissolubly attached to affirmative action. In the distance between the unabashedly racial preferences of affirmative action and the nonracial preferences of such policies as seniority (which function today as racial preferences regardless), white resentment takes root. They may disproportionately gain from other systems of preference, but the hostility of many whites (and some people of color) becomes fastened on the openly racial benefits affirmative action grants to certain racial groups. Affirmative action's focus on redressing the legacy of past racism gets lost amid the myriad cries of unfairness and "reverse racism" constantly leveled against it. And whatever moral weight the principle of affirmative action might possess to counter its opponents has largely been lost, because, as we shall see in our analysis of the most prominent case in the history of affirmative action, that principle no longer operates in the minds of those who support it.

The Trials and Tribulations of Abigail Fisher's Predecessor, Allan Bakke

As the long-term impact of *Fisher v. Texas* on affirmative action cannot yet be predicted with certainty, the most influential case involving affirmative action remains the 1978 Supreme Court case *Regents of the University of California v. Bakke*. The *Bakke* case fundamentally altered the terrain of affirmative action, both in its scope and its rationale. As such, a detailed analysis of *Bakke* deepens our understanding of affirmative action and the spectrum of arguments in support of or opposition to it.

A brief history of the case: in 1973, Allan Bakke, a 33-year old white male, applied to the medical school at the University of California at Davis. After being rejected, he applied the following year and was again denied admission. He sued the UC system, alleging "reverse discrimination." Specifically, the target of Bakke's ire was the "quota" system that the UC Davis medical school had put in place as a means to ensure the presence of racial groups that had previously been excluded (in this regard, the program was fully invested in the principle of affirmative action). Of the one hundred students admitted every year, sixteen of the slots were quotas—spaces that could only be filled by students of color. Bakke provided data that many of these sixteen students had lower GPA and MCAT scores than he did and thus were less qualified.

In the end, Bakke won the case and secured admission to UC Davis's medical school. The Supreme Court's ruling speaks volumes concerning the vastly divergent perspectives the various justices brought to bear on the place of affirmative action in a racially unequal society. In the majority opinion in Bakke's favor, four of the nine justices argued that the quota system in place at UC Davis violated Bakke's civil rights. The Justices "avoided the constitutional issue of whether a race-conscious affirmative action program violated the Equal Protection Clause [of the 14th Amendment] and concluded that Bakke had been treated unlawfully, in violation of an antidiscriminatory provision of the 1964 Civil Rights Act."[7]

Four of the other justices ruled against Bakke in support of the affirmative action program at UC Davis. They found affirmative action to be fully consonant with the precepts of both the Civil Rights Act and the 14th Amendment, insisting that racial preferences were a necessary ingredient for all racial groups to receive the equal protection of the laws. Arguably the best-known statements defending affirmative action on this score were written by Justice Harry Blackmun, who declared that "In order to get beyond racism, we must take account of race. There is no other way." Blackmun grounded his position in the belief that a nonracial administration of the equal protection clause of the 14th Amendment would open the door to the preservation of white privilege; as he also wrote, "We cannot—we dare not—let the Equal Protection Clause perpetuate racial supremacy."[8]

The ruminations of Justice Thurgood Marshall lend further weight to the case for supporting affirmative action. "The position of the Negro today in America," he wrote in dissent, "is the tragic but inevitable consequence of centuries of unequal treatment."[9] Echoing our discussion in chapter 3, Marshall understood why "equality of opportunity" would not translate into "equality of result." Like Blackmun, Marshall believed that blacks' relative lack of qualifications was a direct function of "centuries of unequal treatment" that only race-conscious measures could successfully vitiate. Here, Marshall placed himself squarely in the company of Martin Luther King, Jr., who wrote in his final book, *Where Do We Go from Here: Chaos or Community?*, "A society that has done something special *against* the Negro for hundreds of years must now do something special *for* him...."[10] In the end, Marshall ultimately could not accept the majority's conclusion "that a university may not remedy the cumulative effects of society's discrimination by giving consideration to race in an effort to increase the number and percentage of Negro doctors."[11] His dissent ultimately points to his dedication to the principle of affirmative action: that "the cumulative effects of society's discrimination" would need to be addressed if a racially equitable society were to be realized in this country.

Lastly, in what became the most enduring opinion in *Bakke*, Justice Lewis Powell ruled against UC Davis (thus granting Allan Bakke victory in the case). However, while the other four justices constituting the majority opined for the wholesale scrapping of affirmative action, Powell argued that such policies remained necessary—if in altered form. In other words, UC Davis could still employ affirmative action policies—but the specific quota system the university utilized would have to be discarded. In the end, Powell proposed the following prescriptions for affirmative action: the use of racial quotas would become illegal (at UC Davis or elsewhere), but race could still be used as a "plus factor." This meant that race could be considered as one factor among many, but universities and businesses were forbidden to "set-aside" spaces for any racial groups as was the case with quotas.

Powell's opinion remains the precedent for affirmative action, not only in the way it revised the practice of affirmative action, but because he also changed its *principle*. Ignoring the dissenting pleas of Thurgood Marshall and Harry Blackmun, Powell maintained that race should factor into admissions and hiring decisions *in the interest of "diversity."* As Powell understood it, without affirmative action-type policies, universities would become predominately white (and, increasingly, white and Asian American). As the diversity rationale went, for Americans to relate and compete on the world stage, they would need exposure to various racial groups in all walks of life, especially in the elite arenas of medical school and law school. The latter was the focus of another major affirmative action case, *Grutter v. Bollinger*, in 2003. As in *Bakke*, the diversity justification dictated the Court's decision to uphold the affirmative action program at the University of Michigan law school.

In *Bakke*, then, the principle of affirmative action underwent a tectonic discursive shift. No longer would the *raison d'etre* for affirmative action be to neutralize the present-day effects of past racial discrimination; rather, its focus would simply be to foster "diversity"—a rather conservative and limited aspiration, as I discussed in chapter 1. A recent *Los Angeles Times* editorial lamented the demise of the original principle of affirmative action and its replacement by the diversity rationale (here, the editors are writing in support of the university's affirmative action program in *Fisher v. Texas*):

> One of the most persuasive arguments for some racial preferences is that the underrepresentation of African Americans in the ranks of the highest-achieving college applicants is inseparable from this country's legacy of racial discrimination. Far from offending the 14th Amendment's

guarantee of equal protection of the laws, such policies are consistent with that amendment's paramount objective of overcoming the effects of slavery.

The problem is that, beginning with the court's 1978 decision in the Bakke case from California, affirmative action has been based on a different rationale: that including students from different backgrounds enhances everyone's educational experience. That "diversity" justification, which looms large in the [Obama] administration's brief, is valid as far as it goes. But it gives insufficient weight to the persistent racial disparities in income and education that continue to put minority applicants at a disadvantage.[12]

As the editors note, assertions fashioned in favor of affirmative action today lack cogency, because they largely ignore the continuing impact of past racial discrimination on the life chances of racial groups.

Yet even a further analysis of *Bakke* itself exposes some of the unsolved debates surrounding affirmative action. For instance, in addition to the sixteen seats set aside for minority applicants, the UC Davis medical school reserved five spaces for the children of wealthy donors (an example of yet another preference system).[13] Furthermore, as an individual in his mid-thirties, legal scholars allege that Bakke would have had a greater chance of winning had he sued for *age* discrimination, since medical schools heavily favored twenty-somethings who had just completed their undergraduate curriculum (indeed, several other medical schools had denied Bakke admission in 1972, citing his age as a factor in his rejection). Such scholars note that Bakke had little to say about the age preferences younger applicants had doubtlessly received (nearly half of the white students admitted to UC Davis over Bakke had lower GPAs).[14] It recalls an earlier point I made in this chapter, drawing on the work of Ellis Cose: preferences abound in our society, but only *racial* preferences become the object of vitriolic opposition. This explains why it is unsurprising that Allan Bakke targeted racial preferences, rather than these other forms of preference that pervade medical school admissions and beyond.

The *Bakke* case also highlights one of the primary arguments leveled against affirmative action: reverse discrimination. In what follows, I explore the idea of reverse discrimination as well as some of the other most prominent arguments crafted in opposition to affirmative action, which will allow us to study angles of the affirmative action debate that have been as yet undiscussed in this chapter.

The Arguments against Affirmative Action

The arguments created in opposition to affirmative action are many and varied, accompanied by a level of sophistication resulting from the intensity by which its rivals seek to refute the policy. What follows below is scarcely an exhaustive list; I have selected an inventory of some of the most common criticisms while discussing their background and connection to other issues that we have analyzed in this book.

REVERSE DISCRIMINATION

We begin this discussion with the reverse discrimination line of reasoning, as it is arguably the most influential of the criticisms of affirmative action. As we've seen above, reverse discrimination (or "reverse racism"—the terms are interchangeable) turns on the belief that whites have now become the victims of racism due to affirmative action programs. In essentially every major court case involving the program, reverse discrimination is front and center of the reasoning of those seeking its demolition, as such discrimination, in their view, stands in violation of the 14th Amendment's equal protection of the laws. Allan Bakke, Abigail Fisher, and many others have formed their cases around precisely this argument—and the Supreme Court has listened and been persuaded by it.

An analysis of the opinions of Justices who oppose affirmative action demonstrates that they evince a great concern over the injury the program allegedly inflicts on innocent white victims—an injury they deem Constitutionally equivalent to the racism of slavery and Jim Crow. In other words, such Justices interpret the reverse discrimination argument quite literally, and not merely as a rhetorical device designed to elicit a visceral reaction. As legal scholar Ian Haney-Lopez notes with unease, such a claim "merits only derision—but for the fact that it underlies contemporary constitutional antidiscrimination law."[15] The Justices speak plainly on this matter; in his opinion striking down an affirmative action plan in the highway construction business (*Adarand v. Pena*, 1995), Justice Clarence Thomas rendered this judgment of Jim Crow laws and affirmative action: "I believe that there is a moral [and] constitutional equivalence between laws designed to subjugate a race and those that distribute benefits on the basis of race in order to foster some current notion of equality... In each instance, it is discrimination, plain and simple."[16] Twelve years later, in the concluding sentence of his plurality opinion in the 2007 case, *Parents Involved* (which struck down race-conscious measures by the Seattle and Louisville unified school districts to promote integration), Chief Justice John Roberts proclaimed, "The way to stop discrimination on the basis of race is to stop discriminating on the basis of race."[17]

Not every Justice concurs with the views of Thomas, Roberts, and others. The expression of their views, however, usually occurs in dissent. Characteristic in this regard is Justice John Paul Stevens's dissent in the aforementioned *Adarand* case; responding to Justice Thomas's contention that the discrimination of Jim Crow and the discrimination of affirmative action are one and the same, Stevens intoned:

> There is no moral or constitutional equivalence between a policy that is designed to perpetuate a caste system and one that seeks to eradicate racial subordination. Invidious discrimination is an engine of oppression, subjugating a disfavored group to enhance or maintain the power of the majority. Remedial race based preferences reflect the opposite impulse: a desire to foster equality in society. No sensible conception of the Government's constitutional obligation to "govern impartially,"...should ignore this distinction.[18]

As in Thurgood Marshall's dissent in *Bakke*, we see echoes of the original principle of affirmative action in Stevens's opinion; the "caste system" at the heart of Jim Crow racism has created the very racial subordination that affirmative action aims to eradicate.

SINS OF THE FATHERS

Threading through much of the argumentation against affirmative action is the belief that whites today are unfairly harmed because they did not participate in—and thus are not personally responsible for—the racial oppression of the pre-civil rights US. The common lines, "The past is the past" and "I didn't own any slaves" are everyday expressions of this belief.[19] This is specifically *why* whites are deemed "innocent" by the Court, as pointed out above: even if we acknowledge the "sins of the fathers"— whites in the past who devoted themselves to racial oppression—whites today should not shoulder the burden of those past sins. Abigail Fisher, for example, is not someone who has "personally" discriminated against people of color and should thus not bear the weight of crimes she did not personally commit.

Such reasoning emerged in Justice Lewis Powell's opinion in *Bakke*; as he put it, in affirmative action there is necessarily a "measure of inequity in forcing innocent persons...to bear the burdens of redressing grievances not of their own making."[20] If the racism occurred several generations ago, why must whites pay the price for it now? Here we encounter overlap with the reverse discrimination argument: in both cases, the axiom, "Two wrongs don't make a right" is in full force.

All this, of course, requires that we ignore the many privileges whites have today as a consequence of those "grievances." Earlier in this chapter, I quoted Charles W. Mills, who noted that whites remain in the driver's seat of society due to the sins of whites in the past (of which its deepest footprint lies in racial wealth inequality, as highlighted in chapter 1.) "So unfairness here," asserted Mills, "is manifest in the failure to redress this legacy, which makes the perpetuation of domination the most likely outcome." The "sins of the fathers" argument thus misses the point of the original principle behind affirmative action: as a tool to *neutralize* the advantages whites possess today because of the racism of their ancestors. The claims by Justice Powell (among others) occlude this context, as they suggest that attempts to rectify the outcome of prior racial domination harms innocent parties—even if such individuals carry with them a wide variety of privileges because of that prior domination. At bottom, the common thread of both the reverse discrimination and the "sins of the fathers" arguments becomes the refusal to acknowledge racial privilege. If whites cannot see (or deny seeing) their advantages, then it makes perfect sense to label affirmative action as unfair. (This, of course, begs the larger question of how and why white privilege has been rendered practically invisible in our society.)

STIGMA/HANDOUTS

While the "sins of the fathers" and—in particular—the reverse discrimination lines of argumentation have formed the backbone of the crusade against affirmative action since its inception, this third area—what I'll call here the "stigma/handouts" argument—is relatively more recent. This argument is also distinguished by the fact that it is commonly invoked by people of color who oppose affirmative action.

The logic behind the stigma/handouts argument is as follows: by bestowing preferences on individuals for the sole reason that they "happen" to be members of an "underrepresented minority" group, affirmative action becomes (like welfare) a system of "handouts." Under this reading, such individuals are given an artificial and undeserved boost because of their racial identity, rather than being assessed solely on their merits. This was one of Abigail Fisher's misgivings of the affirmative action program that she considered to be at the heart of her denial to the University of Texas; as a *New York Times* article on her case described it, Fisher believed "she had lost a benefit that her state's government had decided to distribute on a basis other than merit."[21]

Of course, how, exactly, one defines "merit" has been a subject of debate all its own. Critics assert that objective assessments of merit (the kind lauded by Fisher and her ilk) should themselves be the subject of scrutiny. As such critics point out, for instance, wealthy suburban high schools and underfunded inner-city high schools have differing numbers of honors and Advanced Placement (AP) courses available to students. Since the latter group offer disproportionately fewer of these courses, it hampers the overall GPAs of high-performing students, since they thus do not receive the grade point enhancement such accelerated courses offer. (These sorts of differences formed the rationale behind Texas's Top Ten Percent Plan.)

Whatever the persuasiveness of the debate over "merit" for or against affirmative action, its opponents still view such programs as providing handouts to individuals who are seen as not deserving them. Because of this belief, adversaries of affirmative action contend that it stamps its beneficiaries with a stigma. This stigma causes other students or coworkers to eye affirmative action admits with skepticism. "Did you get in because you *deserve* to be here," they inquire, "or are you here only because you got a 'handout'?" As the argument goes, this causes those who received affirmative action preferences to be wracked with self-doubt about their abilities and qualifications. This explains why people of color who disagree with affirmative action often use this line of reasoning; as black former University of California Regent Ward Connerly put it, affirmative action "perpetuate[s] the self-defeating and corrosive myth that we cannot do it without help from someone else—and all too often we don't even try."[22] Affirmative action, in the view of prominent black conservative Thomas Sowell, undermines "the legitimacy of black achievements by making them look like gifts from the government."[23]

One negative consequence of this is that *all* individuals of underrepresented minority groups suffer from it—whether they secured entry through affirmative action or not. In other words, every black student at a competitive university will be placed under the microscope, even if they had a 4.5 GPA in high school, scored a 2300 on the SAT, and were the student body president of their high school. As a result, such individuals will be forced to parry charges of having obtained entry by means other than their own determination and hard work.

And, importantly, this stigma only haunts the beneficiaries of *racial* preferences; there is little evidence that students who secure admission through the legacy clause contend with similar questions about their qualifications, either internally or at the hands of others. Former president George W. Bush is a case in point; despite scholastic credentials that were at best average, he was admitted to Yale, riding on the coattails of his influential father and grandfather.[24] (And it is unlikely he faced any doubts about whether he "deserved" to be there on the part of his classmates.) As before, it is only with *racial* preferences that this happens.

CLASS-BASED AFFIRMATIVE ACTION

The above criticisms of affirmative action are usually fielded by conservative individuals politically aligned with the Republican Party. This final instance of opposition to affirmative action, in contrast, is generally the preserve of liberals. In this case, the nature of the opposition lies not in the concept of affirmative action but in the racial preferences embedded within it. Such individuals argue that any preferences that exist should be *class*-based, rather than race-based; they fear that a racial affirmative action passes over poor whites while providing undue benefits to already-privileged middle-class and wealthy people of color.[25] In brief, they agree that "something" needs to be done to address the many inequities afflicting our society, but they disagree with the employment of racial preferences as a means to that end.

Those clamoring for a class-based affirmative action rarely deny that racial inequality remains a potent problem in US society today; they argue that race-conscious measures of combating it are perilous and prone to backfiring (due to their awareness of the unpopularity of racial preferences among large segments of the polity.) Their fear, as scholars have pointed out, is political in nature—a fear that embracing racial preference will drive away too many white (and some nonwhite) voters, making the practice too politically costly. (Indeed, this fear has gripped politicians since the birth of affirmative action in the 1960s; Daniel Patrick Moynihan, a figure with whom we became acquainted in chapter 3, immediately expressed his profound reservations with racial affirmative action, instead supporting policies aiming to lift "all" poor people out of poverty.)[26]

In the final analysis, an investment in class-based affirmative action requires one to contest Harry Blackmun's aforementioned declarations in *Bakke*, that "In order to get beyond racism, we must take account of race. There is no other way." For them, there *is* another way—one rooted in class. As the reasoning goes, class-based affirmative action will benefit blacks and Latinos more anyway, since they disproportionately inhabit the ranks of the poor. Critics maintain that such groups possess "unique claims for compensatory treatment"[27] that class-based preferences will not adequately capture. In the end, insisting on a class-based affirmative action on the part of the political left becomes the safer strategy, an easy way out that evades the thorny issue of race as a matter of political expediency.

Conclusion

Every time I reengage in a study of affirmative action, I am daunted by the sheer scope of the literature penned in favor of or against the concept. And I am reminded of what I wrote at the outset of this chapter: like racism, covering all the complex dimensions of affirmative action in one short chapter proves an impossibility. Between the history and logistics behind the program—to say nothing of the endlessly polarizing debates surrounding it—any honest analysis of affirmative action becomes at best partial, truncated. If anything, stepping into the affirmative action debate is to wander into a perilous minefield.

What does rise up from the complexity is our society's investment in the idea of "merit" as a benchmark. Those who obtain scarce slots at a prestigious university or Fortune 500 company should be those whose merits make them the most deserving and capable candidates. But as I inquired within this chapter, how exactly is "merit" to be defined and measured? Should university admissions officers and hiring managers solely look at objective criteria such as test scores? Or should they take other factors, such as race, into account?

As I have attempted to illuminate in this chapter, our answers to these questions will remain incomplete so long as the many other preference systems—old boys' networks, the legacy clause, and so forth—remain off the radar in the attacks on race-based affirmative action. As these systems produce racial effects of their own (disproportionately benefiting whites due to past racial discrimination), some form of race-conscious effort on behalf of racialized minorities will be necessary as a counterbalancing agent. Whether the specific form(s) affirmative action has taken in its stormy history are the most equitable and reasonable means by which to neutralize the advantages whites continue to inherit remains an open question. If anything, it points to the conclusion that "something" needs to be done to rectify racial inequality. As we shall observe in the chapters to follow, the most effective way to keep racial inequality in place is to do *nothing*—to act as if such inequities are nonexistent. But any attempt to do "something"—as our discussion in this chapter has brought forth—has been met with cries of unfairness, "reverse discrimination," and the like. That, I submit, represents one of the central racial quandaries we face in the 21st Century.

The above, of course, points to one of the most powerful moral arguments sculpted in opposition to affirmative action: the idea that race-conscious policies stand in violation to our nation's ideal of "colorblindness." Quoting (time and again) Martin Luther King, Jr.'s proclamations in his "I Have a Dream" speech that "my four little children will one day live in a nation where they will not be judged by the color of their skin, but by the content of their character," affirmative action's antagonists allege that such policies inevitably preference skin color over character in an assessment of qualification. Colorblindness becomes, then, a powerful mechanism by which to deflect calls for racial justice since (by definition) it requires that the nation do "nothing" to address contemporary racial inequality. Its complex history—and the controversies it produces today—are the subject of the final three chapters of this book.

Questions

In my discussion of the legacy clause, I briefly mentioned that Asian Americans are starting to increasingly benefit from it. Recalling my analysis of the model minority myth in chapter 3, why do you think this is now the case?

Have a conversation with someone outside this class about affirmative action. If they support it, what justifications do they offer? If they oppose it, what line of reasoning do they employ? Is it one of the lines of opposition discussed here, or something else?

What are the two major principles of affirmative action according to this chapter? Which of the two do you find to be more persuasive?

Justice Harry Blackmun argued in his dissent in *Bakke*, "In order to get beyond racism, we must take account of race. There is no other way." Do you agree? Why or why not?

*Threading through this chapter is a discussion of white privilege. I briefly pointed out how white privilege is often invisible to whites. In light of this chapter (and elsewhere), why do you think this might be the case?

As examined in this chapter, seniority, the legacy clause, and old boys' networks are various nonracial preferences—but preferences that still serve to benefit whites. What other examples of these can we find in our nation today? Are there examples of preferences that are nonracial on the surface, but benefit people of color more than whites?

One key issue regarding affirmative action in education involves the place of Asian Americans. While this group has been discriminated against in the past, they have (as a group) succeeded in education. Where do Asian Americans fall into the affirmative action debate?

Is affirmative action the most effective way to eliminate racial inequality? What other method(s) might be more effective?

Why do you think I titled this chapter "The Hysterics of Affirmative Action?"

Chapter 5

Plessy v. Ferguson and the Origins of Colorblindness

Introduction

In his essay "A Dream Deferred: Toward the U.S. Racial Future," sociologist Howard Winant echoes the position of many scholars, including myself: "The reigning racial ideology in our country today is that of colorblindness."[1] Indeed, three years earlier, Evelyn Nakano Glenn made the same claim, couching it in a subordinate clause: "Despite the reigning ideology of *color blindness* that proclaims the irrelevance of race in the contemporary world...."[2] Glenn's offering proves particularly interesting because it communicates the lack of debate about the issue: colorblindness *is* the "reigning ideology" in this country today. That being the case, any discussion of racial theory requires that we give the concept of colorblindness a full treatment, which is my goal in the remaining chapters of this book.

Colorblindness reigns today largely because of the success of the civil rights movement in eliminating legal racial oppression. Many seize on Martin Luther King, Jr.'s words as he proclaimed that skin color should never matter, and they praise the ideology of colorblindness as the welcome antipode to the pernicious color-consciousness of slavery, Jim Crow, and other forms of racist oppression. As I concluded in the previous chapter, opponents of affirmative action trumpet colorblindness in their attacks, billing it as the only political and moral option on the road to racial equality. If racism has been so thoroughly wounding, so the reasoning goes, the immediate and full abandonment of race in society is deemed as the only acceptable alternative. To "see" race, many argue, is to tumble into the same pitfalls that the nation has throughout its history. In this atmosphere, colorblindness is touted as the ultimate racial panacea.

In this chapter and the two following, I'll be taking a decidedly different stance regarding the relationship between colorblindness and racial inequality. Far from representing the ideal mechanism in creating a racially equal world, colorblindness today functions as the ultimate tool by which to safeguard the advantages whites have accrued throughout US history. For reasons these three chapters will illuminate, in the post-civil rights era of "equality of opportunity," colorblindness is the most effective way to preserve white privilege.

It is in this vein, then, that I present the following definition of colorblindness: "An interpretive framework by which racial inequality is maintained, defended, and created anew."[3] As we proceed, we'll see, specifically, how colorblindness helps to defend whites' manifold advantages and keep them secure, which results in the perpetuation of racial inequality in the 21st Century. But colorblindness does not merely freeze racial inequality in place; it actively creates such inequality anew as it interacts with a variety of mechanisms that did not exist in the same form in previous epochs.[4] Colorblind ideology teaches us that the best way to maintain racial inequality in the US today is *to pretend that it isn't there*, in other words, to legislate as if material racial equality already exists in society. Needless to say, this represents a substantially different perspective on colorblindness than those offered by many scholars and politicians as highlighted above.

These final three chapters will explore these various points in depth. Fully outlining the ideology of colorblindness requires that we study the concept from its genesis, which is the central goal of this present chapter. The way the colorblind metaphor entered the US racial lexicon is an absorbing story all its own; it emerged in one of the most infamous Supreme Court cases in US history:

the 1896 decision *Plessy v. Ferguson*, which declared Jim Crow segregation Constitutional. By taking a long and detailed look at this case (as well as the history surrounding it), we can better understand how colorblindness "got its start," as it were. Our intensive analysis of *Plessy* may seem like a lengthy detour, but in analyzing it, we will be better equipped to grasp the tortured logic that has gripped the concept of colorblindness from its stormy beginnings. We'll begin with the historical context of *Plessy*, followed by the arguments the lead attorney, Albion Tourgee, made in his condemnation of Jim Crow segregation. I then focus on the ruling made by the Supreme Court Justices, ending with a discussion of the immediate aftermath of the case. Throughout, my goal is to locate the origins of colorblind racial ideology in the environment of late-19th Century America and how those origins became a preview for how colorblindness would ultimately operate in the post-civil rights era.

Plessy v. Ferguson: The Background

In his acclaimed critique of high school US history textbooks (titled *Lies My Teacher Told Me*), James W. Loewen attacks and counters the "racial progress myth" that dominates the narratives of textbooks in their discussions of racism. The racial progress myth, in short, posits that race relations have been steadily improving throughout US history. As the myth goes, we used to have slavery...now we don't. We used to have Jim Crow...now we don't. In Loewen's view, this story of progress distorts the reality of racism in US history.

The mid-late 1800s—the background to *Plessy v. Ferguson*—provides a case in point. As historians of the era of Reconstruction (the decade-long period following the Civil War) have shown, the condition of blacks greatly progressed after the Civil War ended. Loewen highlights the increased amity between blacks and whites (especially outside the South) in a December 1865 article in the *Chicago Tribune*. In this quotation, the journalists are denouncing the "black codes"—the attempt by many Southern whites to sharply limit the rights of newly-freed slaves: "We tell the white men of Mississippi that the men of the North will convert the state of Mississippi into a frog-pond before they allow any such laws to disgrace one foot of soil over which the flag of freedom waves."[5] Statements such as these communicate the nature of the improvement in the life prospects of blacks.

These improvements are also reflected in the realm of politics. Predictably, no blacks held a political office of any kind in the South prior to the Civil War, but as James McPherson points out, within a few years after the war, blacks represented "about 15 percent of the officeholders in the South."[6] Furthermore, the US government created such organizations as the Freedmen's Bureau, and they passed the 13th, 14th, and 15th Amendments as a means to protect the rights of emancipated slaves against the backlash of the black codes and related devices designed to keep blacks in a second-class, quasi-slave condition. The black codes and other developments (such as the 1865 formation of the Ku Klux Klan) remind us that while whites' views of blacks undoubtedly changed for the better during these years, large segments of the white populace remained unrepentant in their belief in black inferiority.

Blacks' relatively improved standing, historians point out, didn't last very long. The Hayes-Tilden Compromise of 1877 effectively ended Reconstruction, creating a racial backslide that would culminate in the institution of Jim Crow laws over the next several decades, laws given a Constitutional stamp of approval in 1896 in *Plessy v. Ferguson*. This era in US history thus confirms Loewen's judgment of the idea of racial progress: it is a myth. The experience of blacks in the years between slavery and Jim Crow was eloquently captured in 1935 by the influential black historian and sociologist WEB DuBois: "The slave went free; stood a brief moment in the sun; then moved back again toward slavery."[7]

The years spanning 1877 and 1896, then, showcase a rapid devolvement in the prospects of blacks. In the judicial realm, this took the form of Supreme Court decisions that disempowered the post-Civil War Amendments (particularly the 14th Amendment.) In one notable signpost on the road to Jim Crow—the 1883 *Civil Rights Cases*—the Supreme Court argued that 14th Amendment protections did not cover the private realm (giving business proprietors the latitude to discriminate against blacks as they pleased). Related cases further eviscerated whatever safeguards the post-Civil War Amendments had provided to blacks, gutting those Amendments and rendering them increasingly impotent.

In this deteriorating atmosphere came the ascendance of legalized segregation—a practice that came to be labeled Jim Crow. (The specific origins of the name "Jim Crow" are not known with certainty.) As Jim Crow began cropping up throughout the nation (and particularly in the South), a countermovement ensued, spearheaded by blacks and sympathetic whites, to head off the dangers they saw in the practice. While lower court decisions upheld Jim Crow, a certain group in Louisiana was searching for an opportunity to challenge segregation on the national stage, and in the early 1890s, they believed they had found their chance.

In 1890, the state of Louisiana passed the "Separate Car Act," which required whites and blacks to sit in separate train cars during rail travel. The following year, blacks in New Orleans formed a "Citizens' Committee to Test the Constitutionality of the Separate Car Law." They endeavored to have a black individual purposely violate the law so they could challenge the statute in court. After a series of aborted attempts, the committee found the man who would be their test case: Homer Plessy, a thirty-year-old shoemaker living in New Orleans. In the racial parlance of the time, Plessy was an "octoroon"—he was one-eighths black and seven-eighths white (and was by all appearances a white man). With white antiracist judge Albion Tourgee hired to litigate the proceedings, the Citizens' Committee put their plan into action. On June 7th, 1892, Plessy boarded a train headed out-of-state, announced to the train conductor that he was black, and sat in the whites-only car. His arrest resulted in a series of lower court cases unsuccessfully challenging the Constitutionality of Jim Crow segregation, which Tourgee and the Citizens' Committee appealed all the way to the Supreme Court.

Plessy v. Ferguson: Arguments and Ruling

The Supreme Court heard oral arguments in *Plessy v. Ferguson* on April 13th, 1896. No transcripts were produced of the testimony before the Justices; legal historians generally believe that the lawyers patterned their arguments on the briefs they submitted to the Court.[8] One month later, on May 18th, 1896, the Court handed down its decision, declaring Jim Crow segregation a Constitutionally permissible practice. In the 7-1 ruling, Justice Henry Billings Brown wrote for the majority while Justice John Marshall Harlan penned the solitary dissent. (The ninth Justice, David Brewer, recused himself from the case, likely due to the death of his daughter.)

In this section, I closely analyze the brief for the Citizens' Committee composed by Albion Tourgee, followed by the opinions by Justices Brown and Harlan. This examination will not only situate their varying arguments in the context of the Constitution and Jim Crow, but it will also address the question, "What does all this have to do with "colorblindness"?

BRIEF: ALBION TOURGEE

Due to the fame (and notoriety) of *Plessy v. Ferguson*, Albion Tourgee's brief to the Court is regarded as significant. There, Tourgee pursued two major lines of attack in his attempt to demonstrate why Jim Crow was unconstitutional.

The first central argument Tourgee fashioned explains why the Citizens' Committee deliberately chose a black man who could "pass" for white as their test case. Tourgee employed this strategy because he hoped to expose the instability of the concept of "race" itself; as Mark Golub writes, Tourgee argued that "The Louisiana law was unconstitutional...because it required train conductors or other railway employees to make unqualified on-the-spot determinations of a passenger's race without benefit of formal standards, criteria, or procedures to govern the process."[9] In Tourgee's conception, the very idea of "race" should be considered a fiction, toppling all the classifications based upon it, such as those governing Jim Crow. As Charles Lofgren notes, "in the end [Tourgee] argued that race itself was irrelevant to the determination of right, as a matter of law."[10] And, to quote Golub, "Tourgee hoped to render the racial categories demanded by segregation both practically and conceptually incoherent."[11]

Tourgee's second line of assault proves to be more enduring in the debate surrounding Jim Crow and the Constitution. Specifically, Tourgee attempted to demonstrate that Jim Crow violated the 14th Amendment's equal protection of the laws because it stamped blacks with what was called a "badge of inferiority." In other words, Tourgee insisted in his brief that Jim Crow was similar to slavery in that it placed blacks back into a condition of second-class citizenship. Louisiana's Separate Car Act, Tourgee asserted, had nothing to do with the formal "separation" of whites and blacks in public conveyances and everything to do with the power of whites to make whatever racial decisions they desired (with Jim Crow merely representing one mechanism that reflected that desire). Jim Crow thus had, as its core purpose, the intention of degrading blacks and making them inferior.

That Jim Crow was an outgrowth of white racial power features heavily in Tourgee's brief to the Court. In one famous passage, Tourgee attempted to relate the innumerable privileges conferred upon those identified as "white":

> How much would it be *worth* to a young man entering upon the practice of law, to be regarded as a *white* man rather than a colored one?

Six-sevenths of the population are white. Nineteen-twentieths of the property of the country is owned by white people. Ninety-nine hundredths of the business opportunities are in the control of white people. These propositions are rendered even more startling by the intensity of feeling which excluded the colored man from the friendship and companionship of the white man.... Under these conditions, is it possible to conclude that the *reputation of being white* is not property? Indeed, is it not the most valuable sort of property, being the master-key that unlocks the golden door of opportunity?[12]

It might be difficult to appreciate just how radical such assertions were, coming from a white man in an era where fewer and fewer of his fellow whites dared even entertain such views in their minds, let alone openly (indeed, Tourgee's radicalism secured him more death threats than friends, and his refusal to compromise on these very points was likely central to why he never got the opportunity to become a Supreme Court Justice).[13] In this passage, Tourgee elucidates the other side of the "badge of inferiority" argument, declaring that such racial systems as Jim Crow not only demeaned blacks, but granted innumerable privileges to whites. As such, Tourgee demonstrated that "whiteness" itself was something valuable and indispensable—a "master-key" that opened doors of opportunity for whites that were routinely slammed in the faces of blacks.[14]

Because he located the exercise of white racial superiority at the root of Jim Crow, Tourgee contended that the Constitution could have no part of it. There was no place in the law for the color distinctions inherent in Jim Crow, rendering them utterly unconstitutional. To underscore this point, Tourgee employed a metaphor that he had used previously in his career as a judge and author of novels. "Justice is pictured blind," he proclaimed, "and her daughter, the Law, ought at least to be color-blind."[15]

In this simple statement, we witness the genesis of what has since become the most powerful metaphor by which we come to apprehend the problems of race and racism today: colorblindness. Arriving in this context, it should be clear that the definition of colorblindness that I offered in the beginning of this chapter does *not* apply to Tourgee's use of it, here or elsewhere. In his brief to the Court, Tourgee has clearly wielded colorblindness as a weapon to defeat Jim Crow (and in his other writings, he often used the term "color-blind justice" to communicate this view).[16] Colorblindness, in Tourgee's formulation, was the antithesis to the contemptible color-consciousness that lay at the heart of Jim Crow. Tourgee's brief—and his use of the colorblind metaphor within it—passed by the desks of the eight Justices who heard the case. But as we shall see, it only attracted the attention of one of them.

MAJORITY OPINION: HENRY BILLINGS BROWN

The majority in *Plessy v. Ferguson* was not swayed by Tourgee's powerful brief or any of the oral arguments he made in front of them. Aligning Jim Crow segregation with the 14th Amendment's equal protection of the laws, however, still required a justification, and in his majority opinion for the Supreme Court, Justice Henry Billings Brown accomplished just that. Brown's rationalization of Jim Crow, of course, has not withstood the test of history; in an oft-quoted condemnation of Brown's reasoning, Robert J. Harris disparaged the Justice's opinion as "a compound of bad logic, bad history, bad sociology, and bad constitutional law."[17] While our brief study of the opinion here will confirm Harris's appraisal, it should be remembered that Brown's validation of Jim Crow enshrined legalized segregation as the law of the land for over half a century.

Brown had much to say in his opinion (calling upon the areas of logic, history, sociology, and constitutional law that Harris noted with disdain), and he focused most of his energy directly addressing the central Constitutional question at hand: Did Jim Crow segregation violate the 14th Amendment's equal protection of the laws? Brown's answer was invested with the standard approach of discussing the context for the case and drawing upon precedents that involved the 14th Amendment, such as the aforementioned *Civil Rights Cases* as well as lower court cases which validated Jim Crow segregation.

Brown constitutionalized Louisiana's Separate Car Act with the following reasoning: he trained his attention on the concept of "separate but *equal*." While Brown conceded that the Separate Car Act forbade blacks from entering white cars, he pointed out that the same act forbade whites from entering black cars. In short, both racial groups were being treated *equally*, since blacks and whites were equally excluded from each other's train cars. Brown thus drew a direct line between Jim Crow's logic of separate but *equal* and the 14th Amendment's *equal* protection of the laws. As Brown put it, "the only issue made as to the unconstitutionality" of Louisiana's Separate Car Act on the part of Albion Tourgee is that "it requires the railway to provide separate accommodations and the conductor to assign passengers according to their race."[18] As long as the conductor has rightly assigned blacks and whites to their respective cars, Brown asserts here, no Constitutional rights have been violated (Brown ultimately ignored one of Tourgee's main arguments: the possibility that conductors may assign passengers to the wrong cars). Brown continued: "So far, then, as a conflict with the Fourteenth Amendment is concerned, the case reduces itself to the question whether [Louisiana's Separate Car Act] is a reasonable regulation...."[19] Unsurprisingly, Brown found the act a reasonable regulation on the part of the state and argued that it was not inconsistent with the 14th Amendment.

Yet Brown added more to his reasoning that directly addressed the arguments that Albion Tourgee had crafted in his brief (gratuitously inserting what Harris termed earlier "bad sociology"). Brown the Justice became Brown the sociologist, insisting:

> The object of the [14th] amendment was undoubtedly to enforce the absolute equality of the two races before the law, but in the nature of things it could not have been intended to abolish distinctions based upon color, or to enforce social, as distinguished from political equality, or a commingling of the two races upon terms unsatisfactory to either.[20]

Brown shares here his investment in the belief of ineradicable differences between whites and blacks that dominated scientific thinking at this time, a point we visited in chapter 3. If these differences were "real" in the scientific sense, the Constitution could hardly be expected to dissolve them. As he wrote near the end of his opinion, "Legislation is powerless to eradicate racial instincts or to abolish distinctions based upon physical differences.... If one race be inferior to the other socially, the Constitution of the United States cannot put them on the same plane."[21]

The above legal argument led to its logical conclusion. In what is likely the most infamous passage in Brown's opinion, the Justice countered Tourgee and asserted the following: "We consider the underlying fallacy of the plaintiff's argument to consist in the assumption that the enforced separation of the races stamps the colored race with a badge of inferiority. If this be so, it is not by reason of anything found in the act, but solely because the colored race chooses to put that construction upon it."[22] These comments epitomize the ubiquitously negative appraisal visited upon Brown's majority opinion today, and it proves important to appreciate just how destructive these comments were. Brown is basically telling blacks that their view of Jim Crow as inherently inferiorizing is merely a figment of their own imagination—it was something they were making up in their heads, and that had no connection to reality. In the words of Mark Golub, Brown's statement "thus works as a kind of double injury: it constitutionalizes the physical segregation of racial minorities while simultaneously disqualifying minority interpretations of their own lived experience."[23] Brown's remark plainly communicated that in the realm of racial ideas, only the white point of view mattered. Whatever degradation and disgrace blacks experienced at the hands of racial oppression counted for nothing in Brown's perspective.

DISSENT: JOHN MARSHALL HARLAN

Justice John Marshall Harlan's lone dissent deftly exposed the flaws in Justice Henry Billings Brown's majority opinion while advancing a series of important points of his own. En route, Harlan eloquently rebutted Brown's argument in what the majority of legal experts consider one of the most famous dissents in Supreme Court history. Harlan's dissent also reflects the influence of Albion Tourgee's brief, as we shall see in our analysis of it.

Harlan immediately indicates his understanding of the unequal racial power relations residing at the heart of Louisiana's Separate Car Act when he notes the sole exception to the racial restrictions governing it: nurses. Quoting the act, Harlan writes that "Only 'nurses attending children of the other race' are excepted from the operation of the statute."[24] Harlan well knew that while this exception applied "equally" to both races, it was in truth a one-way street. In the South of the late 1800s, if a nurse was a different race than the child s/he was attending, the nurse was always black and the child white, and not the other way around. In other words, Harlan pointed out that when exceptions were made in segregation statutes, they involved situations where blacks were plainly in service to whites. (These sorts of exceptions filtered into other areas; as we saw in chapter 2, while restrictive covenants barred nonwhites from purchasing homes in certain areas, they could still reside there—so long as they were employed by the white owners of the property.)

Highlighting the nurses exception as his starting argument, Harlan ultimately found ridiculous Brown's notion that Jim Crow segregation was somehow a neutral practice because of its moniker "separate but equal." Harlan reserved particular contempt for Brown's contention that blacks had wrongly perceived Jim Crow as stamping them with a "badge of inferiority," an accusation he brought forth multiple times throughout his dissent. In one instance, he made the following claim:

> It is said in argument that the statute of Louisiana [the Separate Car Act] does not discriminate against either race, but prescribes a rule applicable alike to white and colored citizens. But this argument does not meet the difficulty. *Everyone knows* that the statute in question had its origin in the purpose not so much to exclude white persons from railroad cars occupied by blacks as to exclude colored people from coaches occupied by or assigned to white persons.[25]

A bit later, he made a similar point, arguing that the Separate Car Act emerges from the belief "that colored citizens are so inferior and degraded that they cannot be allowed to sit in public coaches occupied by white citizens. That, as *all will admit*, is the real meaning of such legislation as was enacted in Louisiana."[26] Lastly, in another famous passage, he again excoriated Brown and declared that "The thin disguise of 'equal' accommodations for passengers in railroad coaches *will not mislead anyone*, nor atone for the wrong this day done."[27] Harlan, in summary, insisted that no one was going to be fooled by Brown's attempt to dress up Jim Crow in the finest garments and make it appear nice and wonderful. All Harlan did was lecture to his Supreme Court colleagues what everyone in the nation already knew: that Jim Crow had nothing to do with keeping whites out of black cars, and everything to do with keeping blacks out of white cars (and that this action was the unambiguous expression of white racial power).

As is clear from these excerpts (and in the parts I italicized in them), Harlan continually made reference to other people and their understanding of Jim Crow's true design: the plunging of blacks back into a second-class status. Who might Harlan have in mind? Other parts of his dissent clue us in to his target audience. Elsewhere, Harlan wrote of the abolition of slavery and the passage of the post-Civil War Amendments. "These notable additions to the fundamental law," he intoned, "were welcomed by the friends of liberty throughout the world. They removed the race line from our governmental systems."[28] And Harlan feared the reprisal of those same "friends of freedom" if the "race line" were to rematerialize in the form of Jim Crow segregation. Harlan prophetically warned that due to such actions, "the judgment this day rendered will, in time, prove to be quite as pernicious as the decision made by this tribunal in the *Dred Scott* case."[29]

Was Harlan correct in this prediction? As our analysis of the Cold War in chapter 3 should make evident, Harlan forecasted the liability Jim Crow would later become with pinpoint accuracy. As discussed in that chapter, Jim Crow became a serious problem for the government in the years following World War II as the Soviet Union attempted to undermine the legitimacy of the US by highlighting its participation in the racial caste system created by "separate but equal." And today, most commentators agree that *Plessy* is every bit as disreputable as the *Dred Scott* case in its effects on blacks—to say nothing of the way it damaged the reputation of the US.

While Harlan skillfully pilloried Brown's majority opinion, he still needed to delve further and provide a specific *Constitutional* basis for his condemnation of Jim Crow. And it appears midway through the dissent, in its most famous passage:

> The white race deems itself to be the dominant race in this country. And so it is, in prestige, in achievements, in education, in wealth, and in power. So, I doubt not, it will continue to be for all time if it remains true to its great heritage and holds fast to the principles of constitutional liberty. But in view of the Constitution, in the eye of the law, there is in this country no superior, dominant, ruling class of citizens. There is no caste here. Our Constitution is color-blind, and neither knows nor tolerates classes among citizens. The humblest is the peer of the most powerful. The law regards man as man, and takes no account of his surroundings or of his color when his civil rights as guaranteed by the supreme law of the land are involved.[30]

In this all-important paragraph, the influence of Albion Tourgee's brief on Harlan becomes most evident. Because the Constitution is "color-blind," Harlan averred, the color-conscious distinctions structuring Jim Crow stood in stark violation and could not be tolerated. In Harlan's view, all citizens were "equal before the law," an equality denied in the practice of legalized segregation. On this basis, Harlan declared Jim Crow unconstitutional.

A close reading of this passage, of course, reveals much more to this story. The paragraph's opening sentences become our first hint that any appraisal of Harlan as a heroic, antiracist Justice may be mistaken. Before declaring "Our Constitution is color-blind," Harlan first rattled off a series of *racial inequalities* characterizing US society in 1896: whites possessed more "prestige," more "achievements," more "education," more "wealth," and more "power." And, in Harlan's view, whites would maintain this dominance "for all time"—if they held true to the colorblind Constitution. This brings in a crucial observation: as Harlan fashioned it here, simply because different racial groups were equal "before the law" didn't imply that they were equal in other areas; indeed, Harlan had just taken pains to establish that they were *not* equal "in prestige, in achievements, in education, in wealth, and in power." In "the eye of the law," all citizens experience equality before the colorblind Constitution, which forms the cornerstone of the "constitutional liberty" to which Harlan referred. But this did not commit him to promoting equality in any other area.

What Harlan has done here (as did Justice Brown before him), as numerous legal scholars have suggested, is to formulate a distinction between the *civil* sphere (where the colorblind Constitution guarantees all racial groups the equal protection of the laws) and the *social* sphere (where inequalities in power, wealth, and so forth existed).[31] As Harlan understood it, just because groups had "civil equality" didn't mean they necessarily had "social equality"; the two forms of equality significantly differed and were not necessary preconditions of one another. In other words, whites and blacks could possess civil equality (equal voting rights, the ability to sit together on train cars, etc.), while lacking social equality (the same levels of education, wealth, and so on). Such a maneuver allowed him to oppose Jim Crow while embracing white dominance "for all time." In the words of law professor Reva Siegel, "the legal [or "civil"] equality of which Justice Harlan spoke *presupposed* continuing social *in*equality."[32] Political scientist Joel Olson echoes Siegel: "Harlan's 'color-blind' defense of civil rights for African Americans, then, sanctions white privilege even as it would bring about formal political [or "civil"] equality."[33]

Central to this discussion is Harlan's application of the colorblind metaphor in structuring these claims; there is little doubt that he picked up the concept from Albion Tourgee's brief to the Court (Harlan's *Plessy* dissent was the one time he voiced the metaphor in his thirty-four-year career as a Supreme Court

Justice). Recalling Tourgee's purpose with the metaphor of colorblindness, what immediately stands out from our examination of Harlan's dissent is that when he proclaimed "Our Constitution is color-blind," he had something *very different* in mind than Tourgee did, in his brief or elsewhere. Harlan's employment of the metaphor, as such, was an *appropriation* of the concept of colorblindness as Tourgee had intended it. For Tourgee, colorblindness was a radical, antiracist notion, brandished as a weapon to slay Jim Crow and any other manifestation of racism. For Harlan, colorblindness meant something completely different: while it would indeed force one to oppose Jim Crow (or any other legal expression of racism), *it would allow whites to maintain their dominance "for all time."* Thus was Harlan able to faithfully assure *Plessy*-era whites that loyalty to the colorblind Constitution would in no way threaten their power or status.[34] (Colorblindness, Harlan professed, would indeed condemn Jim Crow and any other system of racial oppression—but it would also keep whites materially dominant in perpetuity.

From the above, it is clear that the definition of colorblindness I supplied at the beginning of this chapter directly parallels Harlan's meaning behind the concept, and not Tourgee's. Harlan was the first to grasp that colorblindness would be the most effective way to defend, maintain, and create racial inequality anew. However, it suggests something even further about Harlan himself: that in the realm of white domination, Harlan was every bit as "racist" as the other seven Justices comprising the majority in *Plessy*. As Peter Irons points out in his treatise *Jim Crow's Children*, Harlan "had no more desire for 'social equality' with blacks than Justice Brown. He was," Irons continues, "a man of his times, the son of slave owners and a man of superior prestige, education, wealth, and power."[35] This observation is easily (and understandably) missed, since Harlan was, after all, the one Justice to oppose racial oppression in the form of Jim Crow.

As history reveals, Jim Crow proved very effective at keeping whites the master race, just as Harlan desired it. This begs a crucial question: If Harlan was every bit as interested as the other Justices in maintaining white dominance, why not simply support Jim Crow as they did instead of crafting an entire dissent vying for a colorblind Constitution? The answer to this question, in fact, was provided earlier. Looking beyond the confines of the US to the international arena, Harlan knew that Jim Crow would fundamentally tarnish the US's image abroad—exactly as it did during the early years of the Cold War. With graceful elegance, Harlan repeatedly inveighed that Justice Brown's attempt to advertise an untainted image of Jim Crow "will not mislead anyone"—least of all an international community for whom the US was supposed to represent a beacon of freedom and hope. Jim Crow, in Harlan's view, functioned as a deadweight the nation was better off abandoning. Harlan was essentially pleading (in vain) to the other Justices, "Jim Crow is simply a bad idea—and since whites are going to be dominant either way, we should just get rid of it." In the end, Harlan's regrets revolved around the majority's refusal to acknowledge the racial cost-effectiveness of colorblindness, causing them to miss its ability to retain white domination "for all time" in a way that would keep the US's international image clean.

This extended perusal of Justice John Marshall Harlan's dissent in *Plessy v. Ferguson* communicates the complexity that lies at the heart of the origins of colorblindness. Harlan became the first to realize that state-sponsored racial oppression was not necessary to safeguard the material privileges whites had accrued during the over two hundred year lifespan of slavery. By being "colorblind," whites would have a dependable way to keep their material advantages "in prestige, in achievements, in education, in wealth, and in power" secure.

Conclusion: The Aftermath of *Plessy v. Ferguson*

As history records, few paid any attention to Justice John Marshall Harlan's dissent in *Plessy v. Ferguson*, and the Jim Crow system he unsuccessfully railed against became the Court-sanctioned law of the land for fifty-eight years (when it was overturned in the celebrated 1954 case *Brown v. Board of Education*, which we'll be examining in the next chapter). The lessons Harlan attempted to communicate about the relationship between colorblindness and racial inequality would thus go into a hibernation that would last until that time. And because he was the dissenter in that case, as Brook Thomas notes, "for the most part the country ignored his argument."[36] And after his death, writes biographer Tinsley Yarbrough, Harlan "faded from memory."[37]

Today, most consider *Plessy v. Ferguson* one of the most important cases in the history of the Supreme Court. Few could have predicted this result in 1896, however. While Harlan's dissent was almost completely overlooked, even the majority's opinion was portrayed as being of little consequence, buried as it was on page 3 of the *New York Times* among other railway decisions.[38] As legal historian Michael Klarman argues regarding this point, when one considers the racist pedigree of the

Justices on the Court in 1896 as well as how segregation had rooted itself in the racial fabric of the nation following Reconstruction, "*Plessy* was easy." The only real surprise in *Plessy*, Klarman further comments, was that anyone dissented at all.[39]

The underwhelming reaction to *Plessy* reveals the extent to which racial opportunities for blacks had soured in the years between 1877 and 1896. At the end of the Civil War in 1865, the nation began making unparalleled (if partial) strides to include blacks in the prosperity of the nation. Yet, within a few decades, the idea that blacks were (in Harlan's words) "so inferior and degraded" that they should be segregated in many aspects of public life had become a taken-for-granted assumption. As pointed out earlier, these facts give the lie to the "racial progress myth" that James W. Loewen noted still features strongly in high school US history textbooks. The fifty-eight year lifespan of Jim Crow contained practices that Douglas Blackmon called (in his Pulitzer Prize-winning book) *Slavery by Another Name*; and David Oshinsky titled his book on convict leasing in the Jim Crow South *"Worse Than Slavery."* If *Plessy* had an immediate effect, it was that it provided all the encouragement Southern whites needed to drive Jim Crow deeper into every crevice of society. Soon, whites and blacks lived separate existences "from womb to tomb," from segregated maternity wards to segregated cemeteries. White racial terrorism dominated this period, from the lynchings of over 3,000 blacks (mostly black males) to the myriad policies crafted to block their ability to rise up in the nation—just a handful of which we encountered in chapter 2. And the concept of colorblindness—whether in the sense put forward by Harlan or Albion Tourgee—was nowhere to be found.

But as history also records, Jim Crow did witness its end during the civil rights movement—and with it came the ascendance of colorblind racial ideology. By the end of the civil rights movement, colorblindness had been firmly planted into the racial discourse of the US—so completely, that it became the nation's dominant racial ideology once Jim Crow and other forms of legal racial discrimination had made their exit. Yet, as I suggested above, this colorblindness was not of the kind envisioned by Albion Tourgee; rather it was the colorblindness advanced by John Marshall Harlan in *Plessy*—the kind designed to keep whites dominant "in prestige, in achievements, in education, in wealth, and in power....for all time." Harlan's dissent in turn witnessed a stunning rebirth, moving from almost total obscurity to one of the most influential Supreme Court opinions ever written. How all this happened is the subject of the next chapter.

Questions

What is the difference between "civil equality" and "social equality," and how did Justices Henry Billings Brown and John Marshall Harlan deploy them? Do we see this distinction today?

In chapter 3 [on page 74], I quoted a statement from Douglas Massey. Does Massey's statement confirm or challenge the "racial progress myth" as it operated in the civil rights movement?

As mentioned in this chapter, Albion Tourgee and Justice John Marshall Harlan both made use of the concept of "colorblindness." How did their versions of colorblindness differ? Whose version is more in use today?

How, specifically, did Justice John Marshall Harlan refute Justice Henry Billings Brown's majority opinion? How did he declare Jim Crow segregation unconstitutional?

Albion Tourgee described whiteness as a "master-key." Does whiteness still function in this way in the 21st Century? Why or why not?

Chapter 6

The Road from Jim Crow to Colorblindness

Introduction

In a memorial for former Supreme Court Justice Thurgood Marshall in 1993, US district judge and longtime colleague Constance Baker Motley shared the following testimony about Marshall's career in the years leading up to the 1954 case *Brown v. Board of Education*:

> Marshall had a "Bible" to which he turned during his most depressed moments....Marshall would read aloud passages from [Justice John Marshall] Harlan's amazing dissent. I do not believe we ever filed a major brief in the pre-*Brown* days in which a portion of that opinion was not quoted. Marshall's favorite quotation was, "Our Constitution is color-blind."...It became our basic creed. Marshall admired the courage of Harlan more than any other Justice who has ever sat on the Supreme Court. Even Chief Justice Earl Warren's forthright and moving decision for the Court in *Brown* did not affect Marshall in the same way. Earl Warren was writing for a unanimous Supreme Court. Harlan was a solitary and lonely figure writing for posterity.[1]

The influence of Justice John Marshall Harlan's dissent in *Plessy v. Ferguson* would then be cemented into the NAACP's brief in *Brown*, which Marshall and his assistant Robert Carter took the lead in composing: "that the Constitution is color-blind is our dedicated belief."[2] Harlan, whose words of dissent in *Plessy* had been all but forgotten, had been resurrected and promoted to a place of centrality in the fight against Jim Crow.

My analysis in chapter 5, however, suggests that something may be amiss in this story. As we overviewed there, while Harlan indeed opposed Jim Crow, wasn't he ultimately advocating for a colorblind Constitution because he recognized its ability to sustain white domination "for all time"? It opens the possibility that Marshall and the NAACP's decision to make Harlan's dissent a focal point of both their inspiration and their legal strategy may have been in error.

What we do know is that by the time he dissented in the *Bakke* case of 1978, Marshall had rejected the notion that colorblindness would lead the US into the racial promised land. As we saw in chapter 4, Marshall lamented the Court's refusal to "remedy the cumulative effects of society's discrimination by giving consideration to race in an effort to increase the number and percentage of Negro doctors." Such a position indicates that he had gone beyond merely abandoning colorblindness to actively opposing it (and indeed, it was the anti-affirmative action majority in *Bakke* who endorsed colorblind university admissions policies). In short, a concept Marshall had all but worshiped in 1954 had become his enemy by 1978. What explains this transformation?

While I will ultimately answer this question, this chapter is not centrally a commentary on Marshall's potential error in swearing fealty to colorblindness on the path to *Brown*. Nor is it primarily a discussion of the newfound interest in Harlan's dissent during that time (though I will certainly be covering these matters at various points throughout). Rather, this chapter is a story of how those whites who were staunchly devoted to Jim Crow's racial order eventually came around to Harlan's wisdom in his *Plessy* dissent: that colorblindness represented a perfectly effective way to keep whites on top of society. As we'll see, whites who championed legal racism in US society didn't embrace Harlan or colorblindness until they were *forced* to once Jim Crow had met its end at the hands of the civil rights movement. And—importantly—this process did not happen overnight; the road from Jim Crow to colorblindness proved a torturous, decades-long process.

How the above came to pass is the focus of this chapter. We begin with a brief account of the technically "colorblind" policies in place during the Jim Crow era itself. As first analyzed in chapter 2, such legislation as the Social Security Act made no reference to race because of the 14th Amendment, yet such programs still succeeded in privileging whites over people of color. In this first section, I pose the question, Why did those who desired to uphold white domination fail to see what Justice John Marshall Harlan clearly had in *Plessy v. Ferguson*—that color-blindness could work equally well in keeping whites on top of US society? More than this: they missed Harlan's point despite the fact that they were already using colorblindness to great effect in the Social Security Act, the Grandfather Clause, and countless other programs.

That lesson, the remaining sections relate, wasn't learned until the civil rights movement; and even then, as I mentioned directly above, it took decades to fully implant that lesson in the minds of those determined to keep legal racism in place forever. In the second section, we examine one of the early moments in this long passage from Jim Crow to colorblindness: the 1948 case *Shelley v. Kramer*. The reactions to that case present an especially fruitful opportunity to understand how supporters of Jim Crow eventually came to surrender their devotion to legalized segregation—doing so because they began to acknowledge the power of color-blindness in achieving the same objective: white domination. I then move to a study of *Brown v. Board of Education*; like *Shelley*, I am less interested in the details of the case itself than in the various responses to it. Upon the Court's decision, devotees of Jim Crow infamously pledged "massive resistance"—a term that communicated the Herculean lengths to which the white South would go to defy the Court's order to integrate their schools.

As aforementioned, however, Jim Crow did finally breathe its last: whites did eventually surrender "massive resistance." Yet as pointed out above, they did so precisely because they were able to latch on to something else—something called "colorblindness." The final sections of this chapter delve into the specifics of how this transpired. Predictably, the root of this shift lay in the political process, and as such, we will be closely looking at the 1964 and 1968 Presidential elections. In the first instance, Republican candidate Barry Goldwater—running on a Jim Crow plat-form—was soundly defeated by Democratic incumbent Lyndon Baines Johnson, who many then saw as the vanguard of the civil rights movement. Despite their trouncing, just four years later the presidency was handed to Republican Richard Nixon. Comparing the approaches of the Republican Party between Goldwater and Nixon reveals plenty in our quest to properly illuminate the road from Jim Crow to colorblindness.

Lessons Unlearned

In chapter 2, we discussed a spectrum of policies designed to prevent people of color from securing a wide variety of rights. For example, the "Grandfather Clause" had the purpose of keeping blacks off the voting rolls despite the provisions of the 15th Amendment (similar mechanisms, such as literacy tests and poll taxes, were manufactured with the same goal of disenfranchising blacks). The New Deal policies crafted in response to the Great Depression operated in a similar fashion: disallowing maids and farmworkers from receiving the benefits of social security and related forms of relief guaranteed that whites would be the New Deal winners. Yet all these policies were colorblind due to the dictates of the 14th Amendment.

Such maneuvers extended beyond the circumvention of the post-Civil War Amendments. Another vivid example during this period involved the segregation of Mexican American schoolchildren in the Southwest. Like blacks, Mexican Americans endured various forms of racism at the hands of whites, from public settings to the workplace to schools. And while Mexican American children were routinely segregated in education, there was a catch: unlike blacks (and other groups of color), Mexican Americans were classified as "white," which meant that Jim Crow did not formally apply to them. With the apparatus of Jim Crow unavailable, whites who sought to separate their children from Mexican American children in schools had to devise another method to accomplish their desires.

In this instance, whites successfully segregated Mexican American schoolchildren through what came to be called the "language handicap" excuse. As the story went, Mexican Americans' supposed deficiency in English justified their exclusion from white classrooms—and this despite the fact that some of the Mexican American children placed there spoke zero Spanish.[3] While English was undoubtedly not the first language of every Mexican American child, civil rights activists saw right through the shabby pretext that was the "language handicap" rationale. Nevertheless, segregation via alleged language barriers persisted in areas with large Mexican American populations, only experiencing the occasional setback (among the most prominent of these being the 1947 California Supreme Court case *Mendez v. Westminster*, which outlawed the segregation of Mexican Americans in schools). The "language handicap" excuse parallels such mechanisms as the Grandfather Clause in a crucial way: they were all technically race-neutral, but they still produced the effect of propping up legal racial oppression.

These examples (and myriad others) prompt the inquiry: Despite all the evidence one would need as to the effectiveness of colorblind public policy in safeguarding white domination, why did defenders of the racial order indefatigably insist on the need for overt legal racism in the forms of Jim Crow and other racist practices? Again, our analysis of the New Deal policies in chapter 2 points us in the direction of an answer. As we saw there, but for the legal blockade of the 14th Amendment, these policies would have blatantly excluded blacks, no questions asked. Jim Crow America, it must be remembered, was a time when the majority of whites bought into the racist folklore—just like segregation itself, they would have had no qualms seeing people of color openly dropped from New Deal benefits (and often, they were simply "indifferent" to the plight of blacks, as Ira Katznelson pointed out). These various maneuvers—from the Grandfather Clause to the "language handicap" excuse—all possessed what I have elsewhere termed "racial malice aforethought." This concept communicates the idea that in spite of the formal colorblindness of such policies and customs, there was no doubt (and no debate) that they were all brewed in the cauldron of racist hatred. As Justice John Marshall Harlan would have put it, they were "thin disguises," one and all. The difference was that the engineers of these mechanisms made no attempt to camouflage their racist intentions. They merely needed to find ways to circumvent the proscriptions of the various Amendments (and the fact that Mexican Americans were defined as "white")—and they did so in ways which just happened to be colorblind.

Such racial malice aforethought prevented defenders of the Jim Crow racial order from appreciating the potential of colorblindness to maintain white domination just as color-consciousness did. They had neither need nor desire to mask the malice aforethought at the heart of these policies; they simply confronted the various blockades illuminated above. *Colorblindness was nothing more than the means to the end.* And so Harlan's lessons remained unlearned.

As we will observe in the sections to follow, however, whites who supported racial domination did eventually pick up the message lodged in Harlan's dissent. As international and domestic events compelled a fundamental reorganization of race relations in the years following World War II, such whites were forced to abandon Jim Crow and the racial malice aforethought that necessarily accompanied it. This produced a major change in how colorblindness came to be viewed. Whereas colorblindness functioned in the Jim Crow era purely as a means to sidestep such inconveniences as the 14th Amendment, as the civil rights movement gathered steam, those committed to white domination began embracing colorblindness *for its own sake*. They banished racial malice aforethought as far into the background as possible as they publicly sang the praises of John Marshall Harlan and his courageous stand against Jim Crow.

The next section provides an account of how this transpired in one specific aspect of the US: official segregation in housing. What we witness there eventually applied to every area of the country: the rejection of Jim Crow (and its concomitants) and the adoption of colorblindness. As aforementioned, this transition took decades, and while it occurred in fits and starts, it ultimately possessed one common denominator—in each instance, whites did not latch onto colorblindness until they were forced to—once legal racism had met its end. The forthcoming example of housing segregation will illuminate how this took place.

Shelley v. Kramer: A Dress Rehearsal (for Colorblindness)

As with the previous section, we first visited the legal/historical context for *Shelley v. Kramer* in chapter 2: the widespread use of racial "restrictive covenants" to legally obstruct people of color from moving into all-white neighborhoods, particularly in the expanding suburbs. White realtors, along with the Federal Housing Administration (FHA) disseminated these covenants under the conviction that racial homogeneity in neighborhood composition was a necessary ingredient for stability. The overwhelming majority of whites acquiesced to these (and related) practices, as they had bought into the stereotype that the introduction of nonwhites into their neighborhoods would damage their land value. As they saw it, areas primarily populated by blacks did seem to become run-down with filth and unstable families, which provided them all the confirmation they needed to keep blacks out of their communities (and to do so in ways they would have never considered "racist"). Of course, as I related in chapters 2 and 3, these same whites failed to notice the exploitation at the core of these deteriorating mostly black neighborhoods, imploding as they were under the weight of the FHA's refusal to insure mortgages for their homes, which exposed them to such ruinous practices as contract leasing.

Restrictive covenants had come under legal fire throughout their lifespan, and they finally met their match in the 1948 Supreme Court case *Shelley v. Kramer*, which came out of St. Louis. In this case, the Court unanimously argued that restrictive covenants were unconstitutional (notably, only six Justices heard the case—the other three had to recuse themselves out of a "conflict of interest," as they lived in neighborhoods covered by restrictive covenants). This was actually a fairly weak position, since the Court said they simply wouldn't "enforce" them. *Shelley* did not nullify such covenants *tout court*, since they were considered "private agreements" that lay outside the social sphere. The difference here was that restrictive covenants would no longer have the Court's blessing. Because of this, despite the rather weak provisions at the core of *Shelley*, the case still made waves in the real estate business and among civil rights groups.

It is the varying reactions to this case that represent the focus of this section. Initially, civil rights advocates were overjoyed by the result in *Shelley*, as they interpreted it as a landmark victory in the larger fight for racial equality. Conversely, white realtors and defenders of the Jim Crow racial order were horrified by the Court's ruling; they feared that the demise of restrictive covenants would spell doom for neighborhood stability. Within a few years, however, the opinions of the rival groups had completely reversed. Now, it was the civil rights groups who were on the defensive, acknowledging the grim reality that in many ways, *Shelley* had made the circumstances in housing segregation worse, not better. Those vying for racial segregation comprehended this as well, and now they were the ones celebrating their unexpected victory that ultimately emerged from the case. That reversal, I argue here, represents a crucial early moment in the realization that colorblindness was just as effective as race-consciousness in securing the goal of maintaining white privilege.

Let's first look closely at the initial response to *Shelley v. Kramer*. Individuals and groups dedicated to ending residential segregation welcomed the outcome in *Shelley*. In contrast, those committed to maintaining segregation found the Court's decision anathema. In his book, *The Shifting Grounds of Race*, historian

Scott Kurashige relates some of the details behind these reactions: "In winning *Shelley*, civil rights advocates hoped they had eliminated the decisive weapon of those practiced housing discrimination."[4] Of the verdict of segregationists, he asserted, "Not only did they fear the 1948 decision would destroy their livelihood; they also warned that society would unravel without racial covenants."[5]

As Kurashige indicates here, civil rights groups' sentiment of victory centered on how this case encouraged them in their larger fight for racial justice; housing segregation, after all, represented just one part of the web of legal racism characterizing US society in the post–World War II era. Kurashige likewise illuminates the trepidation their opponents experienced as they witnessed the demise of a mechanism they found necessary to the continuance of both neighborhood stability as well as their livelihood: restrictive covenants. In their view, the Court had overstepped its boundaries and interfered in what they considered to be the workings of the "free market."[6] The result, they believed, was bound to negatively reverberate into other areas of society and foment further racial discord.

Such feelings of victory and defeat on the part of the two competing groups, as mentioned earlier, were short-lived. Kurashige notes the basis of this shift on the part of civil rights organizations:

> Commenting on the impact of *Shelley* nearly one decade after the 1948 ruling was released, the [Japanese American Citizens League's] Harry Honda observed, "Racial restrictive covenants have been ruled invalid by the highest courts in the land, but the problem only seems to be beginning as more subtle and sinister forms to circumvent the Supreme Court decision come to life." If contemporary Black and Japanese Americans needed vague descriptions like "insidious" and "subtle" to characterize discrimination, it was largely because it was impossible to pinpoint the single mechanism by which postwar racial segregation transpired.[7]

What ultimately lay at the root of these palpable changes in outlook on *Shelley*?

We can find the answer in what the guardians of Jim Crow discovered about the "subtle" ways residential segregation could be achieved. Prior to *Shelley*, white realtors could attach unambiguous racial restrictions to the title deeds of properties; for example, they could employ such wording as, "The owner of said property agrees not introduce any undesirable racial elements into the neighborhood through sale or rent." Upon the ruling in *Shelley*, such restrictions were declared unconstitutional and could no longer be used. White realtors were thus required to adapt to the new procedures *Shelley* decreed—and as Kurashige points out, it didn't take them long to unearth new schemes to maintain the residential color line in ways that did not offend the dictates of *Shelley*.

What they encountered, in short, was the power of colorblindness in achieving those ends. Often, all it took was the simplest of adjustments; recalling the above example, in the post-*Shelley* era, the wording became, "The owner of said property agrees not introduce any undesirable elements into the neighborhood through sale or rent." All they needed to do was delete the word "racial" from the covenant.

Central to the success of such a shift, of course, was the understanding of whites who resided in areas formerly covered by restrictive covenants—they knew *exactly* what "undesirable elements" meant, that it functioned as a "code word" for blacks (and often other nonwhite racial groups). One could exclude "blacks," or one could exclude "*those* people"—the result was the same. And now, since these new covenants contained no explicit references to race, they were in complete alignment with the *Shelley* decision. In a word, those who practiced residential segregation had discovered how colorblindness could prove most useful in accomplishing their desires (and civil rights groups were provided an early warning sign of colorblindness's racially injurious potential). Prior to *Shelley*, it was obvious how residential segregation was produced: at the hands of mechanisms such as restrictive covenants, which made unambiguous references to race. The cessation of such mechanisms ushered in a new playing field, one in which racial segregation was constructed in "subtle" ways that were no less "insidious" in their race-neutrality.

The aftermath of *Shelley* did not single-handedly promote colorblindness to dominance; the thoroughgoing rejection of legal racism remained a decade and more away. Significant though it was (and is), residential segregation represented just one portion of the larger edifice of racial oppression. Such racism, for example, persisted in the workplace (in "No Chinese Need Apply"-type signs), to say nothing of the countless manifestations of Jim Crow in the South (from drinking fountains to train cars to cemeteries). It would take much longer for colorblindness to make its mark in these other areas, for reasons the upcoming analysis of *Brown v. Board of Education* will detail. Like *Shelley v. Kramer*, the spectrum of responses to *Brown* communicate lessons of their own in regard to the attitudes of white segregationists determined to see that their children would never be educated alongside blacks—and who were convinced that formal, state-sponsored Jim Crow (rather than colorblindness) was the only way to achieve this segregation.

Turning the Tide: *Brown v. Board of Education*

Many view *Brown v. Board of Education* as the fundamental antithesis of *Plessy v. Ferguson* for reasons that go beyond the obvious point that it overturned the *Plessy* decision. While *Plessy* has fallen into irredeemable disrepute, *Brown* stands tall as an affirmation of the basic rights of all Americans regardless of race. While *Brown* is celebrated, *Plessy* is reviled. The NAACP and other civil rights organizations who braved the legal behemoth of *Plessy* are regarded today as heroes in the fight against injustice. A closer look at the case will reveal some of the debates surrounding the case, as well as its role in the shift from Jim Crow to colorblindness. At first, *Brown* becomes less an account of the triumph of colorblindness than a story of the sheer determination of Jim Crow's supporters to maintain segregation by any means possible.

Let's first briefly analyze Chief Justice Earl Warren's unanimous opinion in the case itself. While Thurgood Marshall and Robert Carter deployed colorblindness in their line of attack (drawing directly off of Justice John Marshall Harlan's dissent in *Plessy*), Warren did not base his opinion upon it. Rather, the crux of Warren's verdict rested on the "badge of inferiority" argument that Albion Tourgee had crafted in his brief and that Justice Henry Billings Brown had casually dismissed in his majority opinion. Warren built his ruling around the research of psychologists Kenneth and Mamie Clark, who had conducted a series of famous "doll tests" that documented internalized racism among black children. In the doll experiment, black children were shown a white doll and a black doll and were asked which one was prettier, which one was the bad doll, and so forth. The Clarks found that the black children displayed an overwhelming preference for the white doll—and that segregation in schools intensified this preference. For Warren, this was evidence of a harm that was outright unconstitutional. As he wrote in one of *Brown*'s oft-quoted statements, "To separate [black children] from others of similar age and qualifications solely because of their race generates a feeling of inferiority as to their status in the community that may affect their hearts and minds in a way unlikely to ever be undone."[8] For Warren, the psychological damage nullified any argument that Jim Crow was "separate but *equal*"; even if facilities *were* "equal," the very fact of segregation produced the "feeling of inferiority" that Warren denounced in his opinion. Segregation's legal fate was sealed with Warren's well-known words: "We conclude that, in the field of public education, the doctrine of 'separate but equal' has no place. Separate educational facilities are inherently unequal."[9]

A wide range of responses emerged from Warren's decision. Civil rights groups, predictably, praised the verdict, while others urged a "wait and see" attitude of moderation for the Court's decree.[10] However, among whites in the Jim Crow South dedicated to everlasting segregation, their condemnation of the ruling was swift and immediate. With their anger palpable, they pledged "massive resistance" to the Court's ruling. Coined by Virginia Senator Harry F. Byrd, this term expressed that they would take whatever action necessary to defy the dictates *Brown* had set forth. Some of this history is well-known: the famous images of the Federal Guard escorting the first black students into Central High School in Little Rock, Arkansas (at the order of President Dwight Eisenhower) are etched into the nation's memory of a time we have thankfully left behind. Also familiar is the formation of the White Citizens' Council, established immediately after *Brown*. Viewed by many as little more than a highbrow version of the Ku Klux Klan, the White Citizens' Council employed strong intimidation methods to prevent integration.

Whites displaying "massive resistance" stopped at nothing to keep schools segregated. In a maneuver imitated elsewhere, the Prince Edward County, Virginia school district simply closed down its public school system for five years rather than integrate. Other districts institutionalized their own tactics; many adopted "pupil placement laws" that opened enrollment for students to transfer to any previously all-white school upon approval by the state board. Students of all races were welcome to apply, but (conveniently) only white students were deemed psychologically "fit" for success at those schools. Additionally, many white families removed their children from the public school system and enrolled them in private schools—many of which began receiving state funding as part of their defiance to *Brown*. With these and innumerable other schemes at whites' disposal, it is little surprise that, as a 1960 article in the magazine *Commentary* found, if integration of black children in the South were to proceed at its 1959 rate, "it would take four thousand years for all Southern Negro children to achieve their right to equal educational opportunity."[11] As Martin Luther King, Jr. lamented in 1967, "School desegregation is still 90 percent unimplemented across the land."[12]

Compounding these problems was the lack of specificity on the part of Chief Justice Warren in his *Brown* opinion: while he unambiguously shot down "separate but equal," his verdict remained noticeably thin on the details of how to actually go about integrating schools. He had simply declared school segregation unconstitutional. Partly in response to this absence, a follow-up case occurred in 1955, known as *Brown II*. This second case is important because it did provide some details as to how to implement the original *Brown* decision, responding as they were to the conspicuous uptick in "massive resistance"-type strategies to circumvent their earlier ruling. *Brown II* is best known for the phrase they used as an instruction for how quickly they desired to see school integration: that it should happen "with all deliberate speed."[13]

The problem with such wording, as numerous commentators have pointed out, was that "all deliberate speed" left itself wide open to interpretation. It meant whatever one wanted it to mean, and those pledging "massive resistance" to *Brown* seized on the phrase's flexibility. For them, "all deliberate speed" meant, "We'll hopefully get around to integrating in the next century or so." Both *Brown* and *Brown II* thus lacked the teeth to forcefully carry out the orders lodged within them.

With this level of adamant defiance to *Brown*, one can appreciate why the road from Jim Crow to colorblindness took several decades. Few decisions, wrote Charles Silberman in 1964, "have been more violently attacked and maligned."[14] But *Brown*'s opponents did eventually back down. Daniel Patrick Moynihan had correctly predicted this result in 1965 in the Moynihan Report, discussed in chapter 3; as he asserted in his introduction to the report (speaking here of "massive resistance"), "The effort, no matter how savage and brutal, of some State and local governments to thwart the exercise of those rights is doomed. The nation will not put up with it—least of all the Negroes." As Moynihan pointed out, while blacks stood at the forefront of opposing the "savage" and "brutal" efforts to stymie integration, whites were increasingly becoming less enamored of legal racial oppression. That shift in whites' racial attitudes—especially as they found expression in the political realm—became a key reason why opponents of the *Brown* decision eventually surrendered "massive resistance." The details of that shift represent the focus of this chapter's final two sections.

The Rout of Jim Crow

The tumultuous 1960s witnessed possibly the most thoroughgoing alterations in the racial order in US history. This was the moment of de jure racism's denouement, as Jim Crow and the legal racial oppression characterizing US society were finally defeated. Residues of the now-defunct racial order filtered into the 1970s, but Daniel Patrick Moynihan's forecast held true—the nation was no longer going to "put up with" those recalcitrant individuals and groups desperate to hold on to "massive resistance." By the 1970s, racist organizations like the Ku Klux Klan had been moved to the margins of society, and their atavistic convictions in inherent white superiority became the site of disrespect and the butt of jokes.

As we first overviewed in chapter 3, the Martin Luther King, Jr.-led civil rights campaign of "nonviolence" played a significant role in effecting this shift. Whites (especially outside the South) were horrified by the violence Southern whites visited upon defenseless black adults and children—images beamed nightly into their television sets. By the early-mid 1960s, the tide had clearly turned in favor of ridding the nation of the legal barriers to equality of opportunity, culminating in such legislation as the Civil Rights Act of 1964 and the Voting Rights Act of 1965.

Important for our study here is the changing attitudes of whites as all this was happening in the nation. Recalling our analysis in chapter 3, by the mid-1960s, most whites—again, outside the South in particular—had committed themselves to racial equality in principle (crucially distinct from racial equality in *reality*, as we noted in chapter 1). This change meant that they would no longer support the Jim Crow order—a statement they made with their voting power.

The Presidential election of 1964 became the battleground that would influence (and indicate) which direction the nation was moving in regard to race and civil rights. Running on the Democratic ticket was Lyndon Baines Johnson, who had assumed the presidency the previous year upon John F. Kennedy's assassination in November 1963. Johnson was now firmly synonymous with governmental support for civil rights, having just signed the 1964 Civil Rights Act that July. His opponent was Arizona senator Barry Goldwater, a Republican whose platform was centered on the continuance of Jim Crow. His views were fully aligned with those of Alabama governor George Wallace, who had infamously bellowed in his inaugural address in 1963 "segregation now, segregation tomorrow, segregation forever!"

The results of the election signaled where the nation was headed in no uncertain terms. Carrying only five southern states and his home state of Arizona, Goldwater found himself on the losing end of the largest landslide in US electoral history (no candidate has surpassed the 61.1% of the popular vote Johnson received). Johnson's victory spelled doom for Jim Crow; it was precisely what convinced Daniel Patrick Moynihan that legal racial oppression was finished. At this point, equality of opportunity had been sufficiently embraced that any platform opposing it was certain to fail. For state-sponsored racial oppression, the writing was on the wall, and in their defeat, Republicans acknowledged that only a transformation in their political rhetoric could avert further political disaster for them.

In the 1964 Presidential election, Jim Crow was routed, and to utter even a hint of support for it guaranteed political isolation for the Republican Party. Their resounding defeat prompted a colossal reformation in their approach to race. Like the defenders of residential segregation in the wake of *Shelley v. Kramer*, Republicans understood that they were going to have to forsake their support for overt legal racism. And they discovered the same thing as did the supporters of restrictive covenants: that they could carry their message of maintaining white advantage on the wavelengths of colorblindness. Michelle Alexander summarizes this shift in her book, *The New Jim Crow*. Whites slowly surrendering "massive resistance" eventually came to "the understanding that whatever the new order would be, it would have to be formally race-neutral—it could not involve explicit or clearly intentional race discrimination...Barred by law from invoking race explicitly, those committed to racial hierarchy were forced to search for new means of achieving their goals according to the new rules of American democracy."[15] How they successfully achieved this in four short years is the subject of the final section.

The Ascendance of Justice John Marshall Harlan's Colorblind Vision

In the opening of his book, *The Silent Majority*, historian Matthew Lassiter shares a letter written in 1970 by a white father living in an affluent suburb of Charlotte, North Carolina: "As a member of the silent majority, I have never asked what anyone in government or this country could do for me, but rather have kept my mouth shut, paid my taxes, and basically asked to be left alone."[16] As Lassiter notes, this white father was wrong on an important point: the government *had* done something for him by subsidizing his entry into the suburbs during the New Deal era. In chapter 2, we examined the ways the federal government (via the Federal Housing Administration) laid out the red carpet for whites to obtain prime housing in the suburbs, all the while ensuring that people of color would be left out.

Nevertheless, the misgivings of this white father were typical of the sentiments of millions of other whites like him. This group, which came to be called the "silent majority," became a significant force, and with Richard Nixon and his political acumen at the helm, they helped return the Republican Party to power in 1968, just four years after their clobbering at the electoral polls. The "silent majority," as implied in the above letter, were individuals firmly opposed to blatant racism; certainly many whites such as this father had voted for Lyndon Baines Johnson in 1964. This father represented precisely the type of voter Republicans courted after their defeat that year.

The background to this shift resides in the larger racial changes occurring in the late 1960s. In chapter 3, we analyzed the realization many civil rights leaders and others made: that "equality of opportunity" was not going to lead to "equality of result," which triggered calls for the government to go "beyond civil rights" and actively pursue (in the words of Johnson in his Howard University commencement address in June 1965) "not just equality as a right and a theory but equality as a fact and equality as a result." The hundreds of race riots that ensued in the late 1960s repelled many whites who had supported Martin Luther King, Jr. and the civil rights movement; as the doctrine of nonviolence morphed into black power and chants of "Burn, baby, burn!," whites began abandoning their support for the civil rights movement in droves.

The Republican Party capitalized on these shifts and gave these whites an outlet for their frustrations (such as those aired by the white father quoted above). With the rise to dominance of "cultural survival of the fittest" ideology via the Moynihan Report and the model minority myth, whites could safely blame continuing racial inequality on blacks themselves. This allowed them to resent the demands blacks and others were making on the government (and, presumably, people like themselves) for more comprehensive changes in the racial order. The Republican Party took advantage of these changes—but their losses in 1964 taught them that in catering to the needs of resentful whites, they could no longer speak Jim Crow's language, as too many of them were no longer receptive to blatant racism. What the Republican Party discovered, in short, was precisely what advocates of housing segregation had in the wake of *Shelley v. Kramer*: the power of colorblindness in formulating their claims.

Their confidence in latching onto colorblind rhetoric was grounded in the realization pointed out above: "equality of opportunity" would not translate to "equality of result." After years of "massively resisting" equality of opportunity (and decades of possessing the conviction that legal racial barriers were required to perpetuate white domination), they finally came to recognize what Justice John Marshall Harlan had seventy years earlier: that state-sponsored racial oppression simply wasn't necessary. Recalling one point from chapter 5, white conservatives (following Harlan) figured out that even if racial groups possessed "civil equality," it didn't mean they would automatically come to possess "social equality." As mentioned in previous chapters, by 1964, the demographic pattern of "chocolate cities" and "vanilla suburbs" had largely taken root, and with it, all the (dis)advantages that came along with the territory (both literally and figuratively). They saw millions upon millions of white families (such as those of the white father quoted above) safely tucked away in the suburbs—and countless blacks reaping the consequences of contract leasing and related exploitative mechanisms. With those shifts came *wealth*—by accessing first-rate real estate in the suburbs, whites took hold of the wealth that accompanied it. And as before, most blacks had lost wealth through contract leasing and had precious few opportunities to obtain it. Now, even with housing "fully open" to all racial groups, most people of color were unable to move to the suburbs anyway—not because of racism, but because they lacked the wealth. And with such residential segregation came school segregation, with whites living and going to school in the suburbs and students of color living and attending school in the deteriorating inner cities. In such a climate, *Brown* became somewhat superfluous, which was one reason the Republican Party could feel secure in surrendering "massive resistance"—blacks and whites would largely be attending separate schools with or without legal segregation. As a result, divorcing themselves from Jim Crow became less and less painful for them.

Yet, as we learned in chapter 3, the story hardly ended that easily. Radical groups such as the Black Panthers understood the above as well. The "long hot summers" of the late 1960s witnessed hundreds of major riots and unprecedented demands for the government to go "beyond civil rights" and make "equality of result" reality rather than rhetoric. While the changes emanating from the Moynihan Report and the model minority myth were important, for the Republican party to fully cash in, they needed to portray Democrats as the party bowing down to these demands (through such programs as affirmative action)—and doing so at the expense of folks like the white father who simply wanted to be "left alone" in his vanilla suburb. The Republican Party began developing a language that would reach the hearts and minds of these whites—and no one learned to speak it better than Richard Milhous Nixon.

Nixon, who regularly referred to blacks as the n-word to staff members[17] and considered them "genetically inferior"[18] to whites, positioned himself at the vanguard of these changes. The challenge for Republicans became the following: How do you speak to the disaffections and resentments of whites without sounding like a "racist"? Republicans already had an answer to this question, and it had come in the aftermath of *Shelley v. Kramer*. Advocates of housing segregation realized how simple it was to dodge the dictates of *Shelley* by tweaking their covenants from "undesirable racial elements" to "undesirable elements." Such changes could easily manifest in other areas of society.

Like Nixon, Alabama governor George Wallace was another politician swept up in the changing tide. He presented an early blueprint for others such as Nixon to follow—a blueprint taken from the lessons of *Shelley*. As one of his colleagues put it, Wallace "can use all the other issues—law and order, running your own schools, protecting property rights—and never mention race...But people will know he's telling them, 'A nigger's trying to get your job, trying to move into your neighborhood.' What Wallace is doing is talking to them in a kind of shorthand, a kind of code."[19] In the same way that "everyone knew" precisely what "undesirable elements" was referring to in post-*Shelley* housing covenants (nonwhites), Wallace understood how speaking in racial "code" could allow him to speak to resentful whites in a facially nonracist way. He was able to do this without ever mentioning "black people" (or uttering the n-word, for that matter).

Nixon became the primary political inheritor and benefactor of this shift in racial terminology, and the skill with which he wielded it helped him win the presidency in 1968. He took full advantage of whites' increasingly souring mood towards the civil rights movement in the midst of the riots and other demands. His chief of staff, H.R. Haldeman, illuminated his political strategy thus: Nixon "emphasized that you have to face the fact that the whole problem is really the blacks. The key is to devise a system that recognizes this, while not appearing to."[20] Haldeman encapsulated the racial/political balancing act that Nixon perfected. Black people are the problem, but openly stating this becomes a political headache because most whites have abandoned overt racism and are no longer receptive to appeals to racist sensibilities. So to cure that headache (or to prevent getting it in the first place), you adopt racially "coded" terminology that has race at the center of everything "while not appearing to"—in a word, making political appeals that are *colorblind.*

One of the most effective examples of the above had been part of George Wallace's rhetoric: "law and order." Unsurprisingly, Nixon milked that theme for all it was worth. Many whites perceived the riots of the late 1960s as a fundamental breakdown of a system that they felt should be protecting them, and by running on a heavy law and order platform, Nixon could pledge (again, in racially coded terms) that he was on the side of whites disgusted by the trajectory of the civil rights movement. To again return to the anxieties of the suburban white father, rioting people of color were the problem, while presumably "law-abiding" individuals like himself wished to just be left alone. As Michael Flamm argues, "Nixon tailored his [law and order] argument to appeal to middle-class white voters. . . For the most part, those citizens lived in the suburbs."[21] "In the heated environment of fall 1968," Flamm continues, "it was a persuasive message,"[22] and one that brought Nixon and the Republican Party victory in the presidential election that year.

We can now come full circle and bookend the comments above with those of another white father from North Carolina, who penned the following diatribe in 1968:

> I'm sick of crime everywhere. I'm sick of riots. I'm sick of "poor" people demonstrations (black, white, red, yellow, purple, green or any other color!) I'm sick of the U.S. Supreme Court ruling for the good of a very small part rather than the whole of our society....I'm sick of the lack of law enforcement...But most of all, I'm sick of constantly being kicked

in the teeth for staying home, minding my own business, working steadily, paying my bills and taxes, raising my children to be decent citizens, managing my financial affairs so I will not become a ward of the city, County, or State, and footing the bill for all the minuses mentioned herein.[23]

The same themes emerge: anger at the dearth of "law and order," being made to "foot the bill" for the demands of rioting people of color, and believing that the nation (that is, the Democratic Party) was indifferent to the needs of "decent citizens" like himself. As another quintessential "silent majority" member, Richard Nixon swooped in and spoke to his alienation in colorblind, seemingly nonracist terms. And Nixon could do this confidently, because he (and other white conservatives) had learned that a defense of legal racial oppression was no longer a prerequisite for keeping whites securely in control of the nation. Like Justice John Marshall Harlan before them, they finally understood that colorblind legislation would maintain white domination "in prestige, in achievements, in education, in wealth, and in power...for all time."

Conclusion

You start out in 1954 by saying, "Nigger, nigger, nigger." By 1968 you can't say "nigger"—that hurts you, backfires. So you say stuff like, uh, forced busing, states' rights, and all that stuff, and you're getting so abstract. Now, you're talking about cutting taxes, and all these things you're talking about are totally economic things and a byproduct of them is, blacks get hurt worse than whites..."We want to cut this," is much more abstract than the busing thing, uh, and a hell of a lot more abstract than "Nigger, nigger."[24]

The road from Jim Crow to colorblindness in the civil rights era is a story of how white conservatives were obliged to surrender their insatiable cravings for legal racism as a black-led movement (aided by the Cold War nternational climate) successfully uprooted state-sponsored racial oppression for the first time in US history.

The excerpt quoted above is a piece of that history: it is a statement by well-known Republican strategist Lee Atwater in 1981, explaining to Party operatives how race could be utilized as an instrument to gain or maintain political power at a time when most Americans had rejected de jure racism. It also exposes the racial malice aforethought at the core of such tactics: while their goal remains keeping whites in the front seat of economic and political power, openly spewing out such racist invectives as the n-word is a recipe for political disaster and isolation, as the Republican Party discovered in 1964 with Barry Goldwater and his unabashed platform of white racism decisively defeated. As Nikhil Singh has recently argued, airing openly racist views increasingly produced "diminishing political returns,"[25] and Republican politicians, starting especially in the 1960s, began to overhaul and recalibrate their rhetoric to fall in line with the new "racial order of things" (Mukherjee) that the civil rights revolution had successfully inaugurated. Richard Nixon's presidential victory in 1968 signified the first big step in that direction. The Republican Party continued its renovation, embracing colorblind racial rhetoric more and more tightly—and their strategy ultimately found fruition with the election of the individual many acknowledged as the standard-bearer of the party, Ronald Reagan, in 1980. Their success allowed strategists such as Lee Atwater to look back and confirm that the Republican Party's triumph indeed rested on the exiling of the explicit racism that had governed the approach of politicians prior to the 1960s. Keeping whites dominant, Atwater and other operatives understood, required that appeals to overt racism be driven underground, as too many whites believed in the principle of racial equality—but were simultaneously resentful of attempts to make that principle a reality, as we first discussed in chapter 1. Atwater and his colleagues had discovered how to tap into those resentments in ways that were facially colorblind. And so colorblindness came to dominate the political landscape of race relations in the US.

Upon Reagan's successful election, then, the road from Jim Crow to colorblindness experienced completion; as I related at the opening of chapter 5, colorblindness now reigns as the prevailing racial ideology of the US. The final chapter analyzes the distinctive relationship between colorblindness and racial inequality today. We'll return to the particular definition of colorblindness I provided at the outset of chapter 5—"an interpretive framework by which racial inequality is maintained, defended, and created anew." In particular, chapter 7 focuses on the last portion of that definition: how, specifically, does colorblindness create racial inequality *anew*?

Questions

In this chapter (as well as in chapter 5), we've seen that colorblindness can take many forms. The section "Lessons Unlearned" provided an example of one of those forms. In what ways was that form of colorblindness similar to that which Justice John Marshall Harlan propagated in his dissent in *Plessy v. Ferguson*? In what ways was it different?

In chapter 4, I discussed the concept of white privilege and how it is largely invisible to many whites today. Do we see other examples of this here?

After Barack Obama defeated Mitt Romney in the 2012 election, there was much talk about how Republicans need to alter their strategies, as they continue to fare very poorly among people of color. We briefly covered what Republicans did after their defeat in 1964. In what way(s) might current Republican strategies be similar to what they did after 1964? In what way(s) will it differ?

In a recent essay, Gary Blasi writes the following: "As a matter of cold statistical fact, many of California's public schools more closely resemble those one would expect from the era of *Plessy v. Ferguson* than those promised by *Brown*."[26] From our analyses in this chapter, why might this be? How is it related to the surrendering of "massive resistance"?

Chapter 7

The Benign Neglect of Colorblindness

Introduction

Daniel Patrick Moynihan, as much as he may have tried, could not seem to avoid controversy during his tenure as a White House cabinet member. As chapter 3 described, the unintended publicization of the Moynihan Report in 1965 unleashed a polarizing furor; some denounced the report and accused him of "blaming the victim" by daring to suggest that blacks were themselves responsible for their inability to attain "equality of result" (rather than highlighting the destructive effects of racism, poverty, and inner city isolation upon the black family). And others were thrilled with the Moynihan Report, as it implied a "do-nothing" strategy that released whites (along with their inherited privileges) from any culpability or responsibility in the persistence of racial inequality.

Five years later—and now in President Richard Nixon's cabinet—Moynihan found himself at the center of another dispute that mirrored the uproar over the Moynihan Report. In a memo to Nixon—which, like the report, was not intended for the public eye—Moynihan fussed over the worrisome directions the civil rights movement was headed in the late 1960s. He sounded some of the same notes that had embellished the Moynihan Report, emphasizing the growth in the black community of both out-of-wedlock births and female-headed households living in poverty. Moynihan also voiced his paramount concern over Black Panther-type militancy and the "anti-white feeling[s]" exhibited by them along with others in the black community. As a result of such sentiments, these groups were facing intense repression at the hands of conservatives, which only multiplied Moynihan's inventory of fears.

Viewing these racial divisions as fundamentally retrogressive, Moynihan ended his memo to Nixon with the words that would become the source of his latest controversy. "The time may have come," he declared, "when the issue of race could benefit from a period of 'benign neglect.' The subject has been too much talked about. The forum has been too much taken over to hysterics, paranoids, and boodlers on all sides. We may need a period in which Negro progress continues and racial rhetoric fades."[1] As historian James Patterson informs, "Nixon loved the memo, underlining his copy and scribbling 'I agree' over the words 'benign neglect.'"[2] Moynihan, however, did not win the same accolades once the memo was leaked to the press and became public. Patterson relates the reaction from the left: "Many black civil rights leaders and liberals leapt on the phrase 'benign neglect' and accused him of advocating the abandonment of efforts to promote racial justice."[3] As Linda Faye Williams later noted, the phrase itself was "an oxymoron: can neglect ever be benign?"[4]

The "benign neglect" memo ultimately had no direct effect on the Nixon administration's racial policy.[5] Similar to the Moynihan Report, however, the tenor of the memo bolstered the confidence of conservative political operatives who wished the civil rights movement (and especially its radical exponents) would quietly fade away into nothingness. While the fate of Jim Crow still hung in the balance in 1965 at the time the Moynihan Report became public, this was not so with the "benign neglect" memo in 1970, as by then, the fact that Jim Crow was on the outs was a foregone conclusion. At this point, most conservatives had definitively rejected legal racial oppression and embraced the doctrine of color-blindness, making Moynihan's notion of "benign neglect" enormously attractive for them.

I open this final chapter with the "benign neglect" debacle because, in the words of Linda Faye Williams, it "seemed to capture the political spirit of the post-civil rights era."[6] And animating that spirit was the deepening conviction among conservatives (and many others) that colorblindness would be the political ideology of choice in constructing racial policy. When Moynihan wrote of "benign neglect," he unwittingly took a page straight out of Justice John Marshall Harlan's dissent in *Plessy v. Ferguson*. As chapters 5 and 6 related, Harlan contended that colorblindness would allow whites to safeguard their inherited racial privileges. We might consider one of the lines from Harlan's "our Constitution is color-blind" paragraph in light of Moynihan's recommendation that the Nixon administration "benignly neglect" the plight of blacks: "The law regards man as man, and takes no account of his surroundings or of his color when his civil rights as guaranteed by the supreme law of the land are involved."

By 1970, of course, all racial groups possessed the civil rights of which Harlan spoke. But he also insisted that equality before the law had no direct bearing on whatever "surroundings" in which different American citizens happened to find themselves. Previous chapters have provided the details of those differences: while whites had safely fled to their "vanilla suburbs" during the New Deal era, erstwhile racist mechanisms trapped people of color in "chocolate cities." As noted before, these differences in surroundings were not simply geographic; while the suburbs were equipped with superior infrastructure and investments in such resources as schools, the inner cities were facing escalating desolation and destitution as jobs and opportunities escaped to the suburbs and overseas (and for those inner cities, the infusion of drugs was a scant few years away). All this was precisely what Harlan had in mind, as he knew that simple possession of civil rights (or "equality of opportunity") would scarcely dent these differences in "surroundings" that would prove central to the ability of whites to hold onto their privileges and pass them down to the next generation.

Harlan would have fully approved of Moynihan's stance of "benign neglect." It may have been neglect, but it was *benign*—a necessary antidote to the "malign oppression" characterizing the Jim Crow regime that Harlan found so repelling. Considering the congruent enthusiasm of conservatives towards the "benign neglect" memo and the doctrine of colorblindness, it comes as little surprise that Harlan's popularity shot through the roof during these same years. So influential were Harlan's words that President Ronald Reagan's solicitor general Charles Fried could proudly boast of his influence on the administration in the 1980s. "Aside from the white-supremacist caveats," Fried said, Harlan "offered a pretty good slogan for this part of the Reagan Revolution."[7] Of course, Fried erred in naming Harlan's list of white advantages "caveats," as I made clear in chapter 5; on the contrary, Leslie Carr argues in his book *"Color-Blind" Racism*, they ultimately follow Harlan's "caveats" exactly: "that the best way to maintain the domination of the White [race] is to follow the color-blind constitution in all matters of law."[8]

But how, precisely, does colorblindness re-create racial inequality today? As a tool of "benign neglect," colorblind racial ideology requires that the government ignore racial differences (in income, prison rates, *surroundings*, and so forth). By doing so, whites safely carry privileges with them in the 21st Century, from their greater levels of wealth to the advantages we tabulated in chapter 4: seniority, access to old boys' networks, the legacy clause, and countless other mechanisms. I am particularly interested in drawing our attention to some of the specific debates and episodes of the present day—for instance, the recent subprime loan crisis— and showcasing them as examples of how colorblind racial ideology creates racial inequality anew.

The four sections of this chapter critically evaluate a wide array of contemporary issues and link them to colorblindness. The first section explains how colorblindness discounts the influence of pre-civil rights racism upon the patterns of racial inequality that surround us today. The second and third sections are both concerned with the dilemma of "unconscious racism"; my argument will be that colorblindness denies that such unconscious racial bias has any impact on our society, which allows their racially harmful effects to go unchecked (the third section specifically focuses on the Supreme Court's role in this). Finally, in the fourth section, I analyze the recent crisis of subprime loans and the wave of home foreclosure that followed in its wake; I contend that the colorblind treat-ment given to this episode has prevented many from seeing how it created racial inequality anew due to its disproportionate impact on black and Latino families. Collectively, the sections of this chapter seek to render colorblindness and its role in reproducing racial inequality more intelligible. They will show that we are far from living in a so-called "post-racial" society of multicultural harmony.

For the proponents of colorblindness, a much different story emerges. As they point out, the nation is in a much better location with regard to race and racism. A black president—all but unthinkable in the 1960s (or Reagan's 1980s, for that matter)—is now in his second term. Interracial marriage is on the rise, and the nation's youth are growing up in a nation where legal racial segregation has never been part of their lives. The question ultimately becomes one of "how" to most effectively address persisting racism. Do we achieve our colorblind nirvana by being colorblind *now*, or do we follow Justice Harry Blackmun's pronouncements from *Bakke*, that "In order to get beyond racism, we must take account of race. There is no other way"? As our many discussions to this point make evident, my bets remain on Blackmun's counsel. The sections below attempt to demonstrate why.

The Splitting Off of Racial History

In the transition from the civil rights movement to the post-civil rights era, the US shifted from a society based on legal racial oppression to one formed around a colorblind ideal in which race would be ignored or repressed as much as possible. In this contemporary regime of colorblindness, I argue, enduring inequities between racial groups become all but impervious to critique. Disregarding such racial differences become the ideal means by which to keep whites in the front seat of economic and political power. Considering the sincere devotion by which well-meaning Americans trumpet this ideal, why do the results become so racially odious? To answer this question, we need to closely explore the specific effects of colorblind racial ideology.

This section analyzes one such effect: what I will call here (borrowing from Nikhil Singh) the "splitting off of racial history."[9] Colorblindness, I maintain, splits off racial history and renders it irrelevant. What does this mean? We see a piece of it at work in some of the common statements whites articulate when challenged on their racial views: "The past is the past"; "I didn't own any slaves." Such comments capture the splitting off of racial history in important ways. It is not a species of "Holocaust denial"; to split off racial history is not to insinuate that such events as slavery and Jim Crow never occurred. Nor is it to claim that pre-civil rights racial oppression (in whatever form) was something other than destructive and an embarrassment to our national history.

The splitting off of racial history, rather, banishes such embarrassments safely into the past. To split off racial history is ultimately to argue that *the racial policies of the past have no effect on the racial patterns of the present.*[10] Such lines as "The past is the past" mesh with the splitting off of racial history because it implies that whatever happened in the past has no bearing on race or racism in the present. Nikhil Singh relates some of the consequences this produces in racial dialogue: "Today, to see antiblack racism as something that still generates social inequalities marks one at best as oversensitive, with suspect judgment, and at worst as racist, still invested in an invidious logic of race."[11]

The "social inequalities" of which Singh speaks become one ineluctable outcome of the insistence on colorblindness. As I have attempted to relate in essentially every chapter of this book, we cannot properly explain the presence of racial inequality (what I called above "the racial patterns of the present") without looking squarely at the past—to the countless racial policies of the past and their influence upon the contemporary racial order. This is what colorblindness would have us do: to disconnect the impact of slavery, Jim Crow, and the multitude of related policies upon the differing life chances of racial groups today—only a fraction of which we have discussed in the preceding pages. To exercise "benign neglect" is a species of the above, as it inevitably includes the neglecting of racial history. The original principle of affirmative action, discussed in chapter 4, also falls by the wayside; if we split off racial history, engaging the present-day effects of past racial discrimination becomes an impossibility (instead, the focus becomes simply fostering "diversity," which requires no appraisal of the past).

Of the various racial inequities we've described in this book, it is *wealth* that becomes the biggest casualty in colorblindness's drive to split off racial history. For as we first examined in chapter 1, racial wealth differences owe much to the past; as George Lipsitz asserted, wealth "is almost totally determined by past opportunities for asset accumulation, and therefore is the one figure most likely to reflect the history of discrimination." In insisting that "The past is the past," the legacy of racial discrimination gets jettisoned from the conversation, and whatever privileges whites reap from inherited wealth flies safely beneath the radar, where it is not seen as a "racial" privilege at all, as Thomas M. Shapiro has argued (we encountered a similar point in chapter 4 in our analysis of seniority, old boys' networks, and the legacy clause).

Yet the negative consequences of the splitting off of racial history go beyond this. When one proposes that the racial policies of the past have no effect on the racial patterns of the present, it removes racial history as an *explanation* for racial inequality today. The inequalities themselves, of course, remain stubbornly among us in the forms we've seen throughout this book. But splitting off racial history commits one to the position that, whatever has produced such inequalities, they are not a function of prior racist oppression.

These insights take us right to the doorstep of another. If one has deleted history as an explanation for racial inequality, *another explanation is going to take its place*. That is, something else is going to fill the void left behind by the splitting off of racial history. And as we first encountered in chapter 3, that explanation most often becomes the "cultural survival of the fittest" rationale. Racial inequality is not a function of "the sins of the fathers," the story goes, but rather the race-blind result of the different cultures and value systems of racial groups. Racial inequality indeed exists—we all see that it does—but how we *interpret* those inequalities becomes another subject altogether, a debate we first broached in chapter 1. If the US's history of racial oppression has not left behind a legacy, then the existence of racial inequality must owe to some other factor: in this case, the "right" or "wrong" culture and values.

The concurrent rise to influence of colorblindness and cultural survival of the fittest ideology in the later years of the civil rights movement thus comes as little surprise. Colorblindness produces a disconnect between racial past and racial present, allowing persisting differences between racial groups to be written off as a function of behavior and morality. One recalls William Ryan's sarcastic rebuttal to the Moynihan Report: "Is it any wonder the Negroes cannot achieve equality? From such families!" Such retorts punctuate our present moment, from stereotypes as "Blacks and Latinos are lazy" to a litany of other unfounded generalizations about the propensity of various racial groups to abuse welfare, commit crimes, and the like. This generates a critical mass of Americans convinced that, if blacks and Latinos would just "get their act together" and stop complaining about racism, things would be going a lot better for them as a group.

Erasing the past in the form of the splitting off of racial history frustrates attempts to accurately portray how previous racism has helped create the countless inequities that swirl around us. This impulse predates the rise of colorblindness. Drawing off Beryl Satter's historiography, we saw how contract leasing decimated the economic prospects of innumerable black families—and how, in order to stay afloat, they worked longer hours and subdivided their homes. This resulted in a scenario of uncleanliness in black areas (due to the higher population densities) as well as an increasing number of unsupervised children. As mentioned in chapter 3, all whites saw were these unseemly results; they failed to acknowledge the exploitation at the core of those black neighborhoods—in a word, that the root of the problem was not black behavior, but white racism. This erasure allowed whites to feel fully justified in keeping blacks out of the suburbs through the use of restrictive covenants and similar strategies.

The dominance of colorblindness has intensified the above impulses. When the model minority myth praises Asian Americans for their supposed "success," it erases the context for their achievements in education: the fact that the 1965 Immigration Act gave unambiguous preference for the already educated and professional. By splitting off that context, it easily leads one to buy into cultural survival of the fittest ideology—that Asian American educational accomplishments source from their value system, not selective immigration policy. The same goes for racial wealth inequality: when whites relocate to nicer neighborhoods, rather than see such improvement in living standards as a function of their unearned transformative assets, it is interpreted as the logical result of their hard work and delayed gratification. As with the model minority myth and the 1965 Immigration Act, the historical context for whites' disproportionate levels of wealth drops out of the discussion (to wit, the policies of the New Deal and the Federal Housing Administration, examined in chapter 2).

It also leads to the next stage: as contract leasing's effects gave whites all the legitimacy they needed to prevent blacks from moving into their neighborhoods, so too the consequences of historical racism form the basis for opposition to attempts to eliminate material racial inequality, from affirmative action to slave reparations. With the legacy of legal racism safely consigned to the dustbin of history, such policies become viewed as unmerited encroachments upon the rights of whites (whether they are "racist" or not). In its cruder manifestations, this takes the form of such assertions as, "Why should *we* help *them*? Look at the way they act!" And if blacks and Latinos get swept up into the orbit of the nation's bloated criminal justice system, they have no one to blame but themselves.

At bottom, the splitting off of racial history fully blocks an accurate and adequate portrayal of the historical roots of contemporary racial inequality. In every case detailed here (and many others), the performance of racial groups is interpreted as the equitable and fair outcome of the effort they have put into their education, their work lives, and so forth. And this has happened because the legacy of racism in the past has been marginalized in our society. In the purview of a colorblind society, the present-day effects of contract leasing, the 1965 Immigration Act, redlining, restrictive covenants, *ad infinitum* have no place.

The Dilemma of Unconscious Racism

Hurricane Katrina will be forever remembered as one of the nation's worst catastrophes: nearly two thousand died, with damage topping eighty billion dollars. This disaster disproportionately afflicted poor blacks, who had little means of escaping the oncoming maelstrom. As broken levees caused the inundation of wide swaths of the city, the days following the devastation of Hurricane Katrina brought forth the images of the overcrowded Louisiana Superdome in New Orleans as well as those of marooned homeowners begging for rescue off their rooftops. The specifically racial aspect of the crisis went beyond the mere fact that blacks bore the brunt of the calamity; many pointed out that the only reason blacks inhabited these areas in the first place was because of the legacy of racism which had confined people of color to poorer areas of US cities (I discussed the specifics in chapter 2). Furthermore, many believed that the government's slow rescue response was due to the fact that most of those affected were black. The argument was that if those harmed by Katrina had been primarily white and middle-class, the government would have acted more swiftly. This argument came to a head most famously in Kanye West's declaration that "George Bush doesn't care about black people."

However one assesses West's biting criticism, there is little doubt that race played a major role in the aftermath of Katrina. One particular episode is worthy of note here, as it connects to the dilemma of unconscious racism that we will be exploring in this section. Many news outlets began running two photographs side-by-side; both featured New Orleans residents chest-deep in water. The first photograph (from the Associated Press) displayed a black man, with the caption "A young man walks through chest-deep floodwater after looting a grocery store in New Orleans." The second photograph (from the Agence France-Presse), which featured two white people, contained the following caption: "Two residents wade through chest-deep water after finding bread and soda from a local grocery store after Hurricane Katrina came through the area in New Orleans..." The source of the controversy, of course, appears in the words "looting" to describe the actions of the black man and "finding" to describe the actions of the two white people—even though they were engaged in the exact same behavior.[12] What explains this difference? Since we can safely assume that this was not a deliberate tactic of racism on the part of either news agency, we must then conclude that the different interpretations of the survivors' behavior stemmed from *unconscious* perceptions of race. That is, stereotypes of (for example) blacks as criminal have saturated our racial discourse so completely that it leads us to consider their actions "looting," while identical actions on the part of whites will be deemed merely as "finding."

To be sure, this is simply a single instance of such a difference. However, these suggestions have been given increasingly robust confirmations in the realm of social psychology. Over the past several decades, social scientists have made great inroads in mapping out the relationship between racism and the unconscious. They have documented, through a great variety of ingenious social and psychological studies, how racial bias operates at the level of the unconscious, and not simply in ways that are easily discernible and visible. Their studies have demonstrated, in the words of Gary Blasi, that "the behavior of real human beings is often guided by racial and other stereotypes of which they are completely unaware."[13]

We visited one of the most famous early experiments related to this realm of study: the "doll experiment" conducted by Kenneth and Mamie Clark. As chapter 5 noted, this experiment became the main bedrock upon which Chief Justice Earl Warren based his finding that Jim Crow segregation in schools was inherently unequal because of its deleterious social effects upon black children. In evincing a clear-cut preference for the white doll over the black doll, the Clarks held that black children had already *internalized* the belief that white was "better." That is, their young psychological make-up already included a racial component that would doubtlessly negatively influence their sense of self as they matured into adults.

It is a point of great consternation for many that the Clarks' study continues to be replicated today. In 2010, Margaret Beale Spencer published her findings from a study that asked white and black children similar questions that the Clarks had in an attempt to target skin color preference. While she found that the black children did display some preference for lighter skin, the white children overwhelmingly associated whiteness with positive things while regarding darker skin in a more negative manner.[14] Spencer's findings are but one of many investigations that reveal the ways racism dwells at the level of our unconscious; this section will document a handful of other experiments that uncover the salience of unconscious racial bias and its effects upon racial groups today.

The larger argument I wish to make here involves the impact of colorblind racial ideology upon the implications of these myriad experiments. I contend that colorblindness effectively blocks any serious inquiry into what these studies suggest; furthermore, it thwarts an adequate understanding of how deeply rooted stereotypes are in this society—so deep, they function at the level of the unconscious. Colorblindness, in the end, guarantees that we will be unable to accurately discern the racial dimensions of our beliefs and thought processes. It produces a situation where people insist that "race doesn't matter" in their lives, when their behaviors and decisions suggest otherwise.

Let's look at some experiments that concisely capture the dilemma of unconscious racism. In his law review article, "Trojan Horses of Race," Jerry Kang describes on such effort:

> Social congnitionist John Bargh asked participants to count whether an even or odd number of circles appeared on a computer screen. After the 130th iteration, the computer was designed to crash, and the participants were told to start over. A hidden videocamera recorded their reactions. Third-party observers then evaluated those recordings to measure participants' frustration and hostility. What neither participants nor observers knew was that for half the participants, a young Black male face was flashed subliminally before each counting iteration; for the other half, the face was White. As rated by the observers, those who had been shown the black faces responded with greater hostility to the computer crash.[15]

What explains this difference? Since the white and black faces were flashed subliminally across the computer screen, the participants did not have sufficient time to "see" them. This experiment compellingly demonstrates that race has indeed rooted itself at the level of the unconscious.

A variety of "shooter bias" studies lends further weight to the presence and influence of unconscious racism. In one such study, Joshua Correll created a video game in which participants encountered both white and black individuals. Some of these individuals (from both groups) were holding a gun, while others were holding non-threatening objects such as a wallet or a cell phone. Participants in the study were instructed to shoot armed individuals while avoiding those who did not have a gun. Correll placed time constraints into the game to see if participants' errors tracked upon racial lines—and this is precisely what he found. Participants were more likely to shoot blacks who were not holding a gun, and they were more likely to mistake a white target as being unarmed, when they were in fact armed.[16]

A diverse skein of experiments like the above produce analogous findings: the presence of unconscious racism that produces the statistically significant results uncovered by the scientists designing them. We need to ask how all this influences real-world relations outside of the controlled research environment. One of the most widely-used approaches to capture unconscious racial bias in society is known as the "audit study." In these experiments' most common manifestations, researchers pair two individuals: identically matched in every way except race (with one individual being white and the other nonwhite, usually black). They are given the same resumes, experience, etc.—even personality coaching so that they act in similar ways. They then go out and look for apartments, attempt to secure job interviews, and so forth.

These audit studies produce similar results across the board: the white individual has more success, being shown more apartments and securing more calls back from prospective employers. Again, researchers target the role of the unconscious; despite identical resumes, employers have unconsciously bought into (for example) antiblack stereotypes that negatively affect blacks regardless of their actual abilities or qualifications. (This is hardly to suggest that none of this racial bias is conscious; undoubtedly, some employers and apartment managers are acting on prejudices they know that they hold, whether or not they would admit this to others.)

How does colorblindness factor into all this? As pointed out earlier in this section, colorblindness foils attempts to capture the influence of unconscious racism upon our society today. Audit studies communicate this difficulty to great effect, as they generate definite racial patterns (the greater success of the white participants therein). Despite their findings, the employers and apartment mangers collectively responsible for bringing this pattern about will each *individually* deny that racism played any role in their decision-making process. That, I submit, is vintage colorblindness.[17] These employers and apartment managers may claim (and indeed, vehemently insist) "I don't see race, just people," but then how can we account for the racial differences audit studies reveal? Such is the snare of colorblindness, as it leaves us little recourse by which to challenge a society wherein such racial distinctions thrive. Even something as simple as our names can bring about the same results; in a widely-cited study, Marianne Bertrand and Sendhil Mullainathan asked, "Are Emily and Greg More Employable than Lakisha and Jamal?" And they discovered the same pattern of the audit studies: the answer to their article question was an unambiguous "yes." Race influences our thoughts and actions at every level, but the doctrine of colorblindness confounds efforts to address that influence.

In further diversifying the audit study, sociologist Devah Pager went one further and designed one of her own, with an important alteration. In this case, she sent out two groups of white and black males, all of whom were given the task to find jobs. In one of these groups, the white and black males had a criminal background, while the other group had no such record. Not only did Pager find that the possession of a criminal record had a more negative effect on the black males, she discovered that white males with a criminal background actually had more success than black males with no arrest history. As before, while such findings strongly indicate the persisting presence of racial bias (much of it unconscious), our investment in colorblindness forecloses any serious investigation into its preeminence and, ultimately, its negative effects upon people of color.

The Supreme Court and the Standard of Racist Intent

The dilemma of unconscious racism is deepened by the fact that the Supreme Court rejects its influence on its jurisprudence. That rejection, I will demonstrate here, represents but another expression of the Court's dedication to the principle of colorblindness (one we have especially seen in our analysis of affirmative action in chapter 4). As I discussed directly above, colorblindness stymies efforts to detect and appreciate the role the unconscious plays in racial bias. We will see below how the Court gives unconscious bias free reign precisely because it disavows it presence. The Court thus becomes complicit in permitting the racial inequalities that inevitably accompany the refusal to acknowledge the impact of unconscious racism. Through an analysis of several prominent Supreme Court cases, we will come to understand how the Court came to adopt this perspective, in addition to why the Court disregards the findings of the types of experiments examined in the previous section.

The relationship between the dilemma of unconscious racism and the Supreme Court becomes most evident with the rise to dominance of what is known as the standard of *racist intent*, which made its judicial debut in the years following the civil rights movement. Under this standard, in order for individuals to successfully claim that they have been a victim of racial discrimination, they must prove "intent," that is, they must demonstrate beyond a shadow of a doubt that another party "intentionally" discriminated against them on the basis of race. Since the intent standard has not always been the precedent, we first need to explore its evolution. Much of that evolution, we will come to find, owes to the changing ideological composition of the Court from liberal to conservative.

Shaped and impacted by the upheavals of the civil rights movement, the Supreme Court of the 1960s and early 1970s was distinctive for its liberalism. During this period, the Court handed down a series of relatively progressive decisions in a wide range of realms, from *Miranda v. Arizona* to *Roe v. Wade*. In the racial domain specifically, the Court signaled at this time its sensitivity to racism as it emerged in society. It repeatedly displayed its lack of patience with racial discrimination and rebuked companies and other entities that were slow to comply with the 1964 Civil Rights Act.

One of the key rulings typifying the Court's liberal stance during these years was the 1971 case *Griggs v. Duke Power Company*. In brief, *Griggs* involved two black males who sued the Duke Power Company in North Carolina, alleging racial discrimination in the hiring process. Even though Duke Power had started hiring on a supposedly "colorblind" basis in 1964 in compliance with the Civil Rights Act (previously, blacks had only been employed in the lowest-paying jobs there), racial inequality pervaded the company, as many blacks applied but few were hired. Central to the plaintiffs' allegations was a test Duke Power began administering shortly after the passage of the Civil Rights Act; their legal team contended that the test was merely a device to circumvent the act's provisions, since few blacks passed it (the test was a prerequisite for eligibility to be hired). In other words, they believed the test was conceived with "racial malice aforethought."

The Court was persuaded by their argument. Viewing the test to be insufficiently related to the requirements of the job, the Justices ordered the Duke Power Company to hire the black plaintiffs forthwith. The importance of this case to our subject is as follows: the Justices focused on the "disparate impact" of the test upon white and black job seekers. They didn't attempt to locate the "racist" person in the company who was responsible for keeping blacks out in violation of the Civil Rights Act. In other words, they didn't concern themselves with whether anyone at Duke Power had the *intent* to discriminate against blacks. The numbers were enough—that is, the racial inequality that resulted from the administration of the test Duke Power had devised was all the evidence the Court needed. From those numbers, they could make an "inference" that racism was operating at some level of the hiring process. Rooting out individual "racist" people and their (un)conscious antiblack bias was not necessary.

This relatively progressive stance didn't last long. Now in the White House, Richard Nixon stacked the Supreme Court with an array of decidedly more conservative Justices, tilting the ideological bent of the bench decisively to the right. The precedents of these earlier liberal decisions—such as the *Griggs* case—would end up on the chopping block. And just a short five years later, the anvil indeed fell upon the precedent established by *Griggs*, in the form of the 1976 case *Washington v. Davis*.

The background to *Washington v. Davis* closely parallels that of *Griggs*; two black males applied to the Washington, D.C. police department and were denied. They took the department to Court, as they believed that racial discrimination lay at the heart of their rejection. They, too, focused on a particular test the department used as part of their hiring process, which blacks failed at much higher rates than whites. In the end, the black males lost their case as the Court found in favor of the police department. Importantly, they lost for the exact same reason the plaintiffs in *Griggs* won their case. This reversal occurred because the Court abolished the precedent in the earlier decision—specifically, that in cases involving racial discrimination, one did not have to prove racist intent. Despite the racial inequalities characterizing the police force in Washington, D.C., the Court insisted that such imbalances alone were insufficient to make an inference of discrimination. Starting with *Washington v. Davis* (which remains the precedent today), individuals charging racial discrimination must now conclusively prove that someone was personally racist towards them: in a word, the case enshrined the standard of racist intent.

One of the most prominent cases following *Washington v. Davis* that directly involved the racist intent standard is *McCleskey v. Kemp*, decided in 1987. This case proves particularly important because it best highlights the relationship between the Supreme Court and the dilemma of unconscious racism. As such, I give *McCleskey* a fuller treatment than I provided for *Griggs* or *Washington v. Davis*.

In 1978, Warren McCleskey, a black male, was convicted of killing of white male police officer during a robbery in the state of Georgia. The prosecution then sought the death penalty, which they successfully secured. McCleskey's defense team appealed the death penalty conviction—an appeal which became the case *McCleskey v. Kemp*. Specifically, they contended that McCleskey's 8th and 14th Amendment rights were being violated because of the racial discrimination they believed infected the exercise of the death penalty.

To make their case, McCleskey's defense team introduced the findings of the Baldus Study, which had analyzed over two thousand death penalty cases in Georgia in the 1970s. Lead researcher David Baldus and his colleagues investigated such cases to see if race exerted any influence upon the likelihood that one would receive a death penalty conviction. They controlled for a wide variety of nonracial variables, such as the specific circumstances, the severity of the crime, and so forth. They found that race significantly affected the probability of whether one would receive a death penalty conviction. Specifically, their data showed that the race of the victim (rather than the perpetrator) had the biggest influence; those who killed white males were over four times more likely to get the death penalty than those who killed black males. McCleskey's defense team argued that since their client had killed a white man, it unfairly exposed him to the racial biases that the Baldus Study had uncovered and thus stood in violation of his 8th and 14th Amendment rights.

The Court rejected their claims, and Warren McCleskey was executed in 1991. The majority opinion in *McCleskey* speaks volumes to its overall investment in colorblindness. While they did not directly challenge the findings of the Baldus

Study, the majority argued that it could not be used as a basis for the allegation of racism in the administration of the death penalty. And they held this position because they were bowing to the standard of racist intent that had been established eleven years earlier in *Washington v. Davis*. In other words, in order for McCleskey to successfully argue that racism was the guiding force behind his death penalty conviction, he would have had to demonstrate (to again employ the cliché) beyond a shadow of a doubt that somewhere along the line—from his arrest to his trials to his conviction—that someone had intentionally discriminated against him personally. Unless he could root out the racist arresting officer, judge, prosecutor, or jury member, McCleskey's claim of racial discrimination would be rendered invalid. He lost his case because he was unable to produce any racist individual who had the intention of personally discriminating against him.

Yet the findings of the Baldus Study remain. Like the various experiments detailed in the previous section, what David Baldus and his collaborators unearthed was the presence of racial bias in the exercise of the death penalty. Since they had carefully controlled for nonracial variables, what they exposed was the operation of race as an independent force influencing who would receive the death penalty and who would not. As Vijay Prashad points out, by not discrediting the Baldus Study itself, the Court was conceding that racial imbalances do appear in various places of society. "The name *McCleskey*," asserts Prashad, "now refers to both the recognition by the state that racism exists in the criminal justice system *and* the refusal of the state to allow it to enter the clemency of the mandarins."[18] (As Prashad implies, these sorts of imbalances exist everywhere in the criminal justice system, from the death penalty to drug convictions to sentencing severity to being granted or denied parole.)

We need to closely inquire what explains the above. The Baldus Study's findings point to a pair of ominous conclusions. The first directly involves the existence of unconscious racial bias—the kind indicated by the many experiments delineated in the previous section. These studies (including Baldus) suggest the possible presence of unconscious racism that infects sentencing decisions. In this instance, the racial imbalances that permeate the criminal justice system are at least in part a function of the stereotypes individuals absorb in US society, stereotypes that associate (in this case) blackness with criminality. These stereotypes are then activated—consciously or unconsciously—in the context of real-world occurrences like those that led to *McCleskey v. Kemp*. The video game experiment cited previously is but one example of how the stereotype of blacks as criminals affects our behavior at an unconscious level, including the decisions we make about who should and should not receive the death penalty.

The Baldus Study points to a second possibility, however (and one that may be working in concert with the first). This possibility directly involves the matter of racist intent. It could be that people *are* consciously aware that they are discriminating against others on the basis of race, but they are *denying* racist motivation. As scholars and others in this vein have demonstrated, concealing one's racist intent is a profoundly easy thing to do. (And with the way Americans look down on "racist" people, we are given all the incentive in the world to deny racist intent.) It came as little surprise that Warren McCleskey's defense team was unable to bring forward any individuals who had personally discriminated against him—no one was going to furnish their Ku Klux Klan membership card (which likely none of them had anyway) or otherwise admit to whatever racial animus they might possess.

The same has proven true of other cases falling under the racist intent standard. Since racist intent is exceedingly difficult to prove, plaintiffs suing for racial discrimination almost never win. With the intent standard, the Court has erected a barrier almost impossible to hurdle. The example of racial profiling in traffic stops demonstrates this to full effect. Despite all the documentation that racial profiling not only exists but is endemic among patrol officers, Courts only acknowledge such discrimination when it is clear and evident. The problem, as Michelle Alexander writes, is that "any police officer with a fifth-grade education will be able to cite multiple nonracial reasons" why they pull someone over.[19] ("I didn't pull you over because you are Latino; I pulled you over because you didn't use your turn indicator at the proper time. Oh, and by the way, can I see your green card?") The sheer abundance of these "nonracial reasons" for one's decisions—even if they are based in racism—makes racist intent enormously simple to hide and equally difficult to prove.

Whether it is a case of unconscious racism or of denying racist intent, the Supreme Court in its colorblindness dodges an engagement with both. By rejecting the existence of unequal racial patterns (as in *Washington v. Davis* and *McCleskey v. Kemp*), the Court has asserted its disavowal of what I termed in chapter 1 the "materialist" tradition. In the eyes of the Court, the only racism that exists is of the "idealist" variety, that is, racism as bald prejudice and malice.

This directly matches the ideology of colorblindness itself: in a colorblind society, racial prejudice must be combated wherever it is found. But by the same token, if racial inequalities saturate the same society, it is not the Court's business to investigate their existence, so long as observable racial bigotry was not their source. The problem, chapter 1 also related, is that racial prejudice and racist people are not necessary to keep racial inequality in place in US society.

Taken together, the above sections help us understand more clearly why racial inequality thrives so effectively in a society faithful to colorblindness in thought and policy. Turning a (color)blind eye to the racial disparities that emerge essentially everywhere in the country, the Supreme Court reduces racism to individual acts of obvious racial hatred. Applying the racist intent standard to its jurisprudence prevents them from acknowledging the many other routes that can be taken to achieve the spectrum of racial inequities that obtain in the US, from wealth to prison rates to whatever forces produced the differences uncovered in the Baldus Study.

In assessing these issues from the opposite angle, it follows that a nation committed to racial justice would take these patterns seriously and would pose honest questions about their source(s) and how to uproot them. Doing so would ultimately expose the bankruptcy of the racist intent standard. It is precisely this bankruptcy that UCLA law professor Gary Blasi has in mind when he writes of the vast racial inequalities characterizing the public school system in California: "we might explain to the million children of color whose futures are slipping away from them that no one really intends them any harm. No one is intentionally depriving them of books or teachers with some minimal training while ensuring that other children have everything they need and more."[20] Blasi shows here how the colorblindness-engineered racist intent standard forecloses any discussion of the role past racism has played in the gestation of California's unequal public school system. There was no "intent" to harm these children of color—all it took, rather, was several decades of "benign neglect."

The Subprime Loan Crisis and the Reproduction of Racial Inequality

The preceding sections have illuminated some of the attributes of colorblindness. By officially refusing to recognize race, colorblindness creates a rift between the pre-civil rights era and our present moment. In so doing, the multitude of privileges that whites possess spill over into contemporary times, becoming virtually immune to critique and reinterpreted as functions of their hard work and motivation to succeed. The advantages stemming from wealth fall especially into this category, as so much of wealth sources from prior generations that have passed their assets along through inheritance. Colorblindness also prevents us from properly discerning unconscious racial prejudice as a force in our society; despite a mound of evidence that illumines the impact of unconscious racism, colorblindness deters an honest appraisal of that impact and how it harms people of color. This is inevitably followed by opposition to anything distantly smacking of race-consciousness, further institutionalizing the belief in colorblind public policy as the only viable and fair practice.

My criticisms of colorblindness, of course, have attempted to expose its manifold flaws. Far from representing a "fair" practice, the persistence of racial inequality is indebted to the doctrine of colorblindness. The Supreme Court's fealty to colorblind jurisprudence, as we examined in the previous section, guarantees that the racial imbalances exposed in such venues as the Baldus Study will be deemed inconsequential, since racism only matters in the form of unambiguous racist intent. More than this: as related in the definition first given in chapter 5, colorblindness does not simply carry inequality along, but recreates it. The recent subprime loan crisis provides an ideal specific example of how this reproduction takes place.

Bolstered by the belief in homeownership as a vital piece of the "American Dream" (a relatively recent phenomenon, as chapter 2 related), in the 1990s such companies as Goldman Sachs began offering what came to be called "subprime loans." These loans lowered the floor of eligibility to obtain a mortgage. This is, individuals and families who would normally be ineligible to purchase a home (due to a lack of income and wealth to use as a down payment, an insufficient credit rating, and so forth) would now have that opportunity. These would still keep homeownership out of the reach of the poorest families, but for those who had previously not quite qualified for a home mortgage, subprime loans became their ticket to enter the ranks of homeowners.

This story ended very badly, as we now know; not only did subprime loans fail to help families participate in the "American Dream," but the foreclosure crisis they precipitated played a major role in the country's calamitous descent into the "Great Recession." This was followed by a series of federal investigations into the practices of Goldman Sachs and other companies in the subprime business, such as Countrywide Financial. Subprime loans are, of course, just that: "subprime," with bad interest rates and other terms that were less than ideal. The main questions at the heart of the official inquiries into the machinations of these companies were: Did they *know* that subprime loans would lead to mass foreclosures? And did they engage in "predatory lending" practices that obfuscated how risky subprime mortgages actually were? The massive profits pulled in by groups trafficking in subprime loans made many individuals and organizations understandably suspicious of their intentions, which became one of the main motivating factors in prompting investigations against them. As economic devastation deluged the nation, Goldman Sachs revealed earnings of over $13 billion in 2009.[21]

We can now consider the chief inquiry at the heart of this section—how the subprime loan fiasco helped to create racial inequality anew. And we can begin by quoting the opening paragraph of David Harvey's 2010 book, *The Enigma of Capital*:

Something ominous began to happen in the United States in 2006. The rate of foreclosures on housing in low income areas of older cities like Cleveland and Detroit suddenly leapt upwards. But officialdom and the media took no notice because the people affected were low income, mainly African-American, immigrant (Hispanics) or women single-headed households. African-Americans in particular had actually been experiencing difficulties with housing finance from the late 1990s onwards. Between 1998 and 2006, before the foreclosure crisis struck in earnest, they were estimated to have lost somewhere between $71 billion and $93 billion in asset values from engaging with so-called subprime loans on their housing. But nothing was done. Once again, as happened during the HIV/AIDS pandemic that surged during the Reagan administration, the ultimate human and financial cost to society of not heeding clear warning signs because of collective lack of concern for, and prejudice against, those first in the firing line was to be incalculable.[22]

As Harvey then notes, "It was only in mid-2007, when the foreclosure wave hit the white middle class..., that officialdom started to take note and the mainstream press began to comment."[23] By then, the problem had spiraled out of control and economic collapse was imminent. Harvey's comments demonstrate the racial core at the root of the catastrophe: the signs were evident, but few noticed them until they began intruding on the white middle class.

Yet what caused black and Latino families to be directly in the path of the subprime mortgage maelstrom? Federal data indicates that they were disproportionately affected by subprime loans, receiving them at three times the rate of whites.[24] One reason for this is that they were more likely to be in the financial demographic that subprime loan corporations targeted: those who were not quite eligible for a standard mortgage loan. And in his book, *How Race Survived U.S. History*, David Roediger explains why this was the case. "The wholesale foreclosures accompanying [the subprime loan] crisis fall in distinct racial patterns," he asserts, "reflecting the lack of resources black and Latino homebuyers bring to the market *because of past discrimination*, and the ways that they are still steered and preyed upon by lenders."[25] Here, Roediger eloquently lays bare the chain of connections. Blacks and Latinos received hazardous subprime loans at greater rates than whites due to the relative lack of resources (especially wealth) that they brought to the homebuying process. And they lacked such resources due to the "past discrimination" they experienced, which prevented them from building sufficient wealth to be able to purchase homes via standard mortgages at the same rates as whites. Such is the peril of colorblindness and the splitting off of racial history—they break this chain of connections, rendering a portrayal of the racial dimensions of the subprime loan debacle impossible. As Roediger points out, the 2008 presidential race (pitting Barack Obama against, in particular, Hillary Clinton and John McCain) was marked by an "absence of any racial and historical framing of the subprime issue."[26]

Whether interpreted as racial or not, the pernicious effects of the subprime loan tragedy upon blacks and Latinos remain; as David Harvey disclosed in the passage I cited above, they lost between $71 and $93 billion in an eight year period. In fact, United for a Fair Economy put that figure higher: $200 billion.[27] Whatever their actual financial loss, the subprime loan crisis created racial inequality anew, as whites suffered relatively less. But the lens of colorblindness inhibits any racial understanding of the differential impacts that crisis had on whites and everyone else. By refusing to investigate the present-day effects of past racism, colorblindness guarantees that the racial inequality our nation has inherited from the days of legal racial oppression will not simply be carried along, but will be actively created anew as it engages with contemporary mechanisms such as subprime loans. This is "benign neglect" carried to its logical conclusion. None of this, to be sure, is designed to undercut the role of racial prejudice in the present; 21st Century residential segregation is achieved not only through a lack of wealth, but (recalling Roediger above) "the ways that they are still steered and preyed upon by lenders." Whether there was any "racial malice aforethought" tainting the subprime practices of Goldman Sachs and other lenders may never be known with certainty (though evidence to that effect existed).

If anything is clear in our exploration of subprime loans, it is their fraternity with previous housing practices that had similarly ruinous impacts on communities of color: redlining and contract leasing, first discussed in chapter 2. Gregory Squires and Charis Kubrin draw the parallel between subprime loans and redlining in a book published in 2006, before the subprime issue had become a nationwide crisis: "After decades of redlining that starved many urban communities of credit and denied loans to racial minorities throughout metropolitan areas, today a growing number of financial institutions are flooding these same markets with exploitative loan products that drain residents of their wealth."[28] Such wealth, as pointed out above, fell right into the coffers of Goldman Sachs and other firms—exactly who Squires and Kubrin have in mind when they describe how subprime loans "deplete the wealth of those communities for the enrichment of distant financial firms."[29]

Subprime loans, in this regard, represent the 21st Century version of contract leasing. Just as the practice of contract leasing triggered the forfeiture of much of the scant wealth blacks possessed in the post-World War II era, subprime loans have also engineered the loss of substantial wealth for black (and Latino) communities. The incubus of predatory lending practices, notes Beryl Satter, pervaded both:

> Like contract sellers, subprime lenders pushed people to take on more debt than they could handle. While contract sellers got away with inflated prices because bank redlining left their customers with

few alternatives, subprime lenders got borrowers to overmortgage themselves by convincing them that prices would only continue to rise—and by working with handpicked property appraisers...Countrywide Financial...became so enamored of the easy profits to be made that it pushed customers into the subprime category, using ruses such as automatically excluding cash reserves when tabulating borrowers' assets.[30]

Similar to contract leasing, black and Latino neighborhoods were targeted, not because they were in redlined communities in which mortgages were completely unavailable, but rather because "minority communities remained underserved by banks, [with] aggressive subprime marketers [being] only too eager to fill the vacuum."[31] Ultimately, contract leasing and subprime loans possessed the same common denominator: predatory lending.

We can conclude by returning to what Satter termed the "subprime loan race gap."[32] Despite their myriad parallels, subprime loans differ on one major point from redlining and contract leasing: while these earlier exploitative practices were transparently racist, the racial effects of subprime loans are often missed (a point David Roediger made earlier, noting that Obama and his competitors made little or no mention of race). We know from the Federal Housing Administration's appraiser's manuals that neighborhood racial composition had everything to do with why inner city communities of color were redlined, as such racial preferences were openly stated in the manuals themselves. This, of course, became the background to contract leasing, in which black families were unambiguously and unabashedly targeted. No doubt existed as to the racist "intent" of the individuals promoting redlining and contract leasing.

Not so with subprime loans. Unlike redlining and contract leasing, the subprime loan episode transpired in today's era of colorblindness. As this chapter has demonstrated, colorblindness detaches the racial dimension of subprime loans, preventing many from appreciating how this crisis disproportionately devastated black and Latino families. Thus, in this Obama-led nation in which many Americans believe racial issues are "getting better," the actual racial impacts of subprime loans provoke a reaction that is decidedly less sanguine, as those impacts represent part of the reason why, on many levels (such as wealth), racial inequality is only worsening.

Conclusion: Towards the (Obama?) Future

Colorblindness could be described as "official government nonrecognition of race." As such, colorblindness signifies the investment in policies that are race-blind. Throughout this book (and especially from chapter 4 forward), we have witnessed the many ways race-neutrality can be harnessed to reproduce white material domination "in prestige, in achievements, in education, in wealth, and in power...for all time." This reproduction can take place through simple "benign neglect," rather than through outward shows of racial force. This chapter has identified a variety of reasons why and how this has been the case.

First, colorblindness has constructed a chasm between history—in particular, the pre-civil rights era—and our contemporary moment. By "splitting off racial history," whites carry with them such unearned inherited advantages as wealth, which helps equip them to maintain hold of their position in the racial structure. That position is reflected in their presence in wealthy neighborhoods with well-funded schools and greater access to quality health care for themselves and their children. Furthermore, by splitting off racial history, whites' position in the racial structure becomes explained by reference to "cultural survival of the fittest" ideology; far from being in part a function of unmerited benefits that have been passed down to them from previous generations, whites prosper today due to their superior cultural capacities, from their appreciation for hard work to their saving habits. The legacy of pre-civil rights racial oppression gets swept away, and the events of those woebegone eras of slavery and Jim Crow become merely artifacts to learn something about in history class.

Colorblindness may signal the government's nonrecognition of race in public policies, but that does not mean that people themselves are ignoring race in their everyday lives. Not only is the recognition of race alive and well in 21st Century US society, race also operates at an unconscious level. As the myriad experiments I detailed in this chapter demonstrate, we (re)act upon racial cues in ways which are not always consciously evident to us. Discounting the effects of such unconscious bias in the social arena as well as in the legal realm (displayed by the Supreme Court's standard of racist intent) guarantees that whites will continue to win out in society—in ways that colorblindness all but renders invisible.

Lastly, colorblindness produces other contemporary effects. As much emphasis as I've placed on the importance of racial history, it's important not to marginalize policies and processes in the present which serve to reproduce racial inequality. Imani Perry makes this point to great effect in her recent book, *More Beautiful and More Terrible*: "I believe we should be historically aware, even humbled by historic knowledge...[However], we must avoid the danger of looking back in order to avoid looking at the present."[33] The subprime loan cataclysm confirms Perry's musings; while such loans have direct antecedents in redlining and contract leasing, their damaging effects transpire in the here-and-now. Even if much of this situation was configured by past racism, new ways of maintaining white privilege are being invented in our midst—ways that do not depend on the presence of overt racists with Swastika tattoos on their arms. As before, not only does colorblind racial ideology prevent us from appreciating the power of such mechanisms as subprime loans to keep most people of color outside the halls of authority and influence, their location there is easily written off as a function of their own personal failings.

The word "most" in the previous sentence reminds us that colorblindness operates in more ways than those enumerated in this chapter. While "most" people of color languish in inner cities, prisons, and the like, "some" others have become fabulously successful, rising even to the highest office in the land. This phenomenon—what is often called the "Obama Effect"—becomes another product of our devotion to colorblindness, as the presence of a small but significant contingent of conspicuously successful minorities fortifies the conviction that racism is no longer a force halting their progress. For many individuals, that a black man resides in the White House cancels any arguments that racism remains a potent impediment to the life chances of people of color.

This tendency to praise wildly successful people of color predates Obama, of course; such figures as Fredrick Douglass[34] and Ralph Bunche[35] have served this purpose in the past. The difference is that Obama has produced an intensification of this idea, rising as he did to the pinnacle of American leadership. As seen in the quotations above, conversations about racism as a blockade to achievement have met their end in this society, and the doors to success are open to anyone with the gumption and the drive to pursue it.

The Obama Effect is a similar (if a more particularized and specific) version of the model minority myth. While the latter praises an entire racial group, the Obama Effect upholds (in particular) black and Latino individuals who have "made it." They both share one important intended effect, however: to discipline the millions of other nonwhites who have not been successful and remain on the socioeconomic fringes of society. "If they've made it, why haven't you?" becomes the inquiry that squelches any insistence that the legacy of pre-civil rights racism might still inhibit the life prospects of people of color today.

All told, colorblindness becomes the ideal ideology of the post-civil rights era. It allows the country to navigate two seemingly opposing realities: a situation where, on the one hand, most Americans denounce racial bigotry, while on the other, racial inequality flourishes as strongly as ever. This, however, becomes the central trap of colorblindness, since not only does it reproduce racial inequality, it does so *under the aegis of antiracism*. In simpler terms, it allows whites to maintain possession of their privileges while at the same time thinking that they are being antiracist. Many Americans sincerely believe that being colorblind in interpersonal interactions and public policy is the fairest way to approach racial issues, given our sorry history of legal racial oppression prior to the civil rights movement. But this same approach guarantees that racial gaps in income, life expectancy, education, and (especially) wealth will persist. Yet many of these same fair-minded Americans insist that attempts to erase these gaps are themselves racist, since they take race into account and violate the colorblind ideal that is held in such high regard. Needless to say, this conundrum has driven our conversations on race into a discursive cul-de-sac, and extricating ourselves from it will prove enormously difficult. How we ultimately deal with this will inform the shape of racism and race relations in the coming decades.

Questions

Where else do we see the destructive effects of "benign neglect"? Why does the concept of benign neglect fit in so well with colorblindness?

Historian Beryl Satter noted that today, banks "underserve" minority communities. While firms peddling subprime loans helped fill that vacuum, in what other ways does the absence of mainline banking companies serve to keep inner city communities poor?

What moral issues emerge from the Baldus Study's findings that killers of white men were given harsher punishments than killers of black men?

Which more accurately explains the findings of the Baldus Study (as well as audit studies in general): unconscious racism or hiding racist intent?

In what way(s) might the "cultural survival of the fittest" ideology help to explain the findings of the Baldus Study and audit studies in general?

Why do you think race went largely undiscussed by politicians as they tackled the subprime loan crisis?

All told, why is colorblindness so effective in helping to maintain racial inequality?

Conclusion

One of Malcolm X's better-known sayings was "Racism is like a Cadillac, they bring out a new model every year."[1] The enduring popularity of this remark stems from the sheer fact of its accuracy; as the seven chapters of this book have attempted to showcase, racism has morphed and altered many times throughout its lifespan. From the unabashed racism of yesteryear (justified through reference to religion or biology) to the cautious and veiled "colorblind" racism of today (justified through reference to culture and values), the concept of racism has doubtlessly taken on a diverse number of models in its ignominious history.

The timing of Malcolm X's truism—the early 1960s—comes as little surprise, for at that moment, the very meanings of race and racism were transmogrifying in unparalleled ways. Both Malcolm X and Martin Luther King, Jr. (among many others) sensed that the backlash to the civil rights movement was manufacturing the latest model of racism; the pair understood in their later years that racism possessed a "staying power" that did not depend on legal systems of oppression such as slavery and Jim Crow for its sustenance and upkeep. Following Malcolm X, scholars have described racism as the "changing same"—surely it has undergone undeniable modifications over the centuries, but its core remains the same: enrichment and protection for some, degradation and destitution for many others.

If racism has changed before, we can be certain it will change again. It is, of course, impossible to predict with any certainty how racism will be expressed and justified in the coming decades; as chapter 3 related, the fact that equality of opportunity did not produce the expected outcome of equality of result initially took Malcolm X and Martin Luther King, Jr. by surprise. Over the past several years, scholars have taken on the task of identifying trends that can help to highlight where the nation is headed in its relationship with the race concept.

Among the most common observations is the forecast that by the year 2050 (if not earlier), whites will become a numerical minority in the US. This situation already exists in such states as California and Texas, where people of color outnumber whites. Owing to the substantive changes ushered in by the civil rights movement, many of the rising number of nonwhites in the nation are entering positions of influence in politics, academia, the media, and elsewhere. Such shifts, some scholars argue, may very well "blur the color line" and tilt the balance of power in the coming years.[2] And as stated at various points in this book, accelerating levels of intermarriage are transpiring alongside this growing racial diversity in the US. How an increasing number of interracial Americans might alter the discourse of race relations in this country remains a point of potent speculation.

Also important in assessing how race and racism might change is a focus on the nation's youth, as their views will eventually rise to influence as they become adults. A new generation is growing up—one that will have no knowledge of a time when the idea that a person of color could become president was considered far-fetched if not impossible. For many in America, that fact, in conjunction with the expanding presence of people of color in influential political and economic posts as pointed out above, may indeed widen the horizons of what is possible in this country for individuals of any racial group. Despite the continuing existence of palpable racial gaps from the university to Madison Avenue, shifting demographics might potentially usher in changes in the racial order, dissolving stereotypes and allowing marginalized groups to take advantage of increasing opportunities.

Alongside these optimistic conjectures, of course, is the much more guarded assertion that race relations could deteriorate, carrying ever-higher levels of inequality with it. In chapter 5, we discussed the falsehood that race relations have steadily improved throughout US history. This "racial progress myth" possibly lurks behind the portraits of sanguinity that the racial future will be one of increasing amity and equality, rather than increasing division and inequity.

To caution that race relations could potentially worsen is by no means an assertion bathed in cynicism and disillusionment. We live in the post-civil rights era: the era of colorblindness. The later chapters of this book showed what colorblindness is capable of—extending racial inequality infinitely into the future, all the while writing off the struggles of people of color as owing to their own defective values and culture. The post-civil rights era is also the era of racial wealth inequality, a time in which the power of wealth in (re)producing racial inequality is on full display, as whites have vastly disproportionate access to the transformative potentials of wealth, helping them pass down their inherited racial advantages to the next generation. Any discussion of where race relations might lead in the coming years must take these and other developments into full and sober account.

In 2009, then-Attorney General Eric Holder accused the populace of the US as being a "nation of cowards" in the way we deal with racism in this country. Whether we agree with Holder or not, the many arguments of this book make certain that cowardice cannot usher in a post-post-civil rights era of racial equality; it will take steady doses of courage and resolution to eradicate the many barriers that stand in the way of racial justice and a new era of racial peace for this nation.

Endnotes

Introduction

1 Tracie Egan Morrissey, "Racist Teens Forced to Answer for Tweets about the 'Nigger' President." http://jezebel.com/5958993/racist-teens-forced-to-answer-for-tweets-about-the-nigger-president.Online. Accessed 1 April 2013.

2 "Mapping Racist Tweets in Response to President Obama's Re-election." http://www.floatingsheep.org/2012/11/mapping-racist-tweets-in-response-to.html.Online. Accessed 1 April 2013.

3 Quoted in Mackenzie Weinger, "Bill O'Reilly: 'The White Establishment Is Now the Minority.'" http://www.politico.com/blogs/media/2012/11/bill-oreilly-the-white-establishment-is-now-the-minority-148705.html.Online. Accessed 1 April 2013.

4 See Michael B. Katz, *The Undeserving Poor*.

5 See Tali Mendelberg, *The Race Card*.

Chapter 1

1 Sara Gates, "Tonya Battle, African American Nurse, Sues Michigan Hospital for Race Discrimination." http://www.huffingtonpost.com/2013/02/16/tonya-battle-hurley-medical-center-race-discrimination_n_2702373.html.Online. Accessed 1 April 2013.

2 Annie-Rose Strasser, "New York City Cop Testifies That He Was Told to Target Young Black Men." http://thinkprogress.org/justice/2013/03/22/1761621/black-men-stop-frisk-recording/Online. Accessed 1 April 2013.

3 Jeff Karoub, "Tanya Battle, Michigan Nurse's Discrimination Suit Reveals Medicine's 'Open Secret.'" http://www.huffingtonpost.com/2013/02/22/tanya-battle-michigan-nurse-discrimination-suit_n_2744546.html.Online. Accessed 1 April 2013.

4 Paul D'Amato, *The Meaning of Marxism*, 23.

5 Ibid.

6 Ibid.

7 Ibid, 25.

8 Ibid, 23-4.

9 Ibid, 23.

10 See "Future of Iraq: The Sp*oils* of War." http://www.independent.co.uk/news/world/middle-east/future-of-iraq-the-spoils-of-war-431114.html.Online. Accessed 1 April 2013.

11 Quoted in Paul D'Amato, *The Meaning of Marxism*, 24.

12 Ibid.

13 *The Oxford Desk Dictionary and Thesaurus*, 654.

14 Elizabeth Anderson, *The Imperative of Integration*, 25.

15 James W. Loewen, *Lies My Teacher Told Me*, 170-1.

16 Melvin Oliver and Thomas M. Shapiro, *Black Wealth/White Wealth*, 108.

17 See Yuval Elmelech, *Trasmitting Inequality*.

18 Melvin Oliver and Thomas M. Shapiro, *Black Wealth/White Wealth*, 154-9.

19 Thomas M. Shapiro, *The Hidden Cost of Being African American*, 60.

20 Ibid, xi.

21 George Lipsitz, *The Possessive Investment in Whiteness*, 14.

22 James W. Loewen, *Lies My Teacher Told Me*, 171.

23 Daniel Rigney, *The Matthew Effect*, 60-1.

24 Thomas M. Shapiro, Tatjana Meschede, and Laura Sullivan, "The Racial Wealth Gap Increases Fourfold."

25 See Frank Wu, *Yellow*.

26 Daniel Rigney, *The Matthew Effect*, 58-9.

27 Stokely Carmichael and Charles V. Hamilton, *Black Power*, 4.

28 Heather Beth Johnson, *The American Dream and the Power of Wealth*, 123.

29 Eduardo Bonilla-Silva, *Racism without Racists*, 54.

30 Charles W. Mills, "Racial Exploitation and the Wages of Whiteness," 48-9.

31 See Michael Awkward, *Burying Don Imus*.

32 See Melvin Oliver and Thomas M. Shapiro, *Black Wealth/White Wealth*, ch. 9.

33 Imani Perry, *More Beautiful and More Terrible*, ch. 1.

34 See George Fredrickson, *Racism: A Short History*.

35 See Dorothy Roberts, *Fatal Invention*.

36 Lawrence Blum, *"I'm Not a Racist, But..."*, 102-3.

37 This definition draws on Lani Guinier and Gerald Torres, *The Miner's Canary*, 43.

38 Stephen Steinberg, *The Ethnic Myth*, 265.

39 See Charles W. Mills, "Modernity, Persons, and Subpersons."

40 See Larry Tise, *Proslavery*.

41 Joe Feagin, *Systemic Racism*.

42 Robert J. Lopez, "Anaheim High School Cancels Events Found to Be Demeaning." http://articles.latimes.com/2012/aug/22/local/la-me-0823-high-school-event-20120823.Online. Accessed 1 April 2013.

43 Rheana Murray, "Penn State Sorority Girls Busted for Offensive Photo at Mexican-Themed Party." http://www.nydailynews.com/news/national/sorority-girls-busted-mexican-themed-pic-article-1.1213746.Online. Accessed 1 April 2013.

44 Russell Goldman, "Duke Students Protest 'Racist Rager' Frat Party." http://abcnews.go.com/blogs/headlines/2013/02/duke-students-protest-racist-rager-frat-party/Online. Accessed 1 April 2013.

45 Ibid.

46 See Shannon Sullivan, *Revealing Whiteness*, conclusion.

47 Quoted in David Ikard and Martell Lee Teasley, *Nation of Cowards*, 7.

Chapter 2

1 Ira Katznelson, *When Affirmative Action Was White*, 22.

2 Ibid.

3 Quoted in Tanner Colby, *Some of My Best Friends Are Black*, 97.

4 Thomas Sugrue, *The Origins of the Urban Crisis*, 45.

5 George Lipsitz, 373.

6 Ibid, 372.

7 Ellen Noonan, "Segregation, In Deed." http://www.nowandthen.ashp.cuny.edu/2010/02/segregation-in-deed.Online. Accessed 1 April 2013.

8 Tanner Colby, *Some of My Best Friends Are Black*, 117-8.

9 David Freund, *Colored Property*, 358; Douglas Massey and Nancy Denton, *American Apartheid*, 45.

10 Douglas Massey and Nancy Denton, *American Apartheid*, 71.

11 David Freund, *Colored Property*, 23.

12 Beryl Satter, *Family Properties*, 4.

13 Ibid, 57.

Chapter 3

1 Martin Luther King, Jr., *Where Do We Go from Here?*, 4.

2 Jack Bloom, *Class, Race, and the Civil Rights Movement*, 1.

3 3See Phil Hutchison, "The Political Economy of Colorblindness," 130; Mary Dudziak, *Cold War Civil Rights*.

4 Leon Litwack, *How Free Is Free?*, 120.

5 James Cone, *Martin and Malcolm and America*, 280.

6 Charles W. Mills, "White Supremacy as Sociopolitical System," 36.

7 Leon Litwack, *How Free Is Free?*, 115.

8   Daniel Patrick Moynihan, "The Negro Family: The Case for National Action."

9   Ibid.

10   Ibid.

11   Lyndon Baines Johnson, "To Fulfill These Rights." http://www.lbjlib.utexas.edu/ johnson/archives.hom/speeches.hom/650604.asp.Online. Accessed 1 April 2013.

12   Ibid.

13   Ira Katznelson, *When Affirmative Action Was White*, 18-9.

14   Lyndon Baines Johnson, "To Fulfill These Rights." http://www.lbjlib.utexas.edu/ johnson/archives.hom/speeches.hom/650604.asp.Online. Accessed 1 April 2013.

15   Eric Sundquist, *King's Dream*, 209.

16   Lyndon Baines Johnson, "To Fulfill These Rights." http://www.lbjlib.utexas.edu/ johnson/archives.hom/speeches.hom/650604.asp.Online. Accessed 1 April 2013.

17   Eric Sundquist, *King's Dream*, 208.

18   Howard Winant, *The New Politics of Race*, 173.

19   Daniel Patrick Moynihan, "The Negro Family: The Case for National Action."

20   Leon Litwack, *How Free Is Free?*, 121.

21   William Ryan, *Blaming the Victim*, 5.

22   Ibid.

23   Beryl Satter, *Family Properties*, 5.

24   David Freund, *Colored Property*, 3.

25   William Ryan, *Blaming the Victim*, 8.

26   Phil Hutchison, "The Political Economy of Colorblindness," 121.

27   Quoted in Timothy Fong, *The Contemporary Asian American Experience*, 63.

28   Quoted in Stephen Steinberg, *The Ethnic Myth*, 272.

29   Ibid. 273.

30   Timothy Fong, *The Contemporary Asian American Experience*, 78.

31   Stephen Steinberg, *The Ethnic Myth*, 79.

32   Ibid, 80.

33   Eduardo Bonilla-Silva and David G. Embrick, "Are Blacks Color Blind Too?", 48.

34   Stephen Steinberg, *The Ethnic Myth*, 80.

35   Lee Rainwater and William Yancey, *The Moynihan Report and the Politics of Controversy*, 11.

36   William Ryan, *Blaming the Victim*, 9.

37   Harvard Sitkoff, *The Struggle for Black Equality*, 155.

38   Douglas Massey, *Categorically Unequal*, 112.

Chapter 4

1   Lawrence Blum, *"I'm Not a Racist, But..."*, 22-3.

2   Ibid, 23.

3   Michael Kinsley, "How Affirmative Action Helped George W." http://www.cnn.com/2003/ALLPOLITICS/01/20/timep.affirm.action.tm/index.html.Online. Accessed 1 April 2013.

4   Charles W. Mills, "Racial Exploitation and the Wages of Whiteness," 41.

5   Ellis Cose, *The Rage of a Privileged Class*, 115.

6   Ibid, 116.

7   Charles R. Lawrence III and Mari Matsuda, *We Won't Go Back*, 51.

8   438 U.S. 407.

9   438 U.S. 395.

10 Martin Luther King, Jr., *Where Do We Go from Here?*, 90.

11 438 U.S. 396.

12 "Affirming Affirmative Action."

13 George Lipsitz, *The Possessive Investment in Whiteness*, 21.

14 Ibid, 36.

15 Ian Haney-Lopez, "'A Nation of Minorities,'" 987.

16 Quoted in ibid, 987.

17 551 U.S. 41.

18 Quoted in John Powell, *Racing to Justice*, 110.

19 Eduardo Bonilla-Silva, *Racism without Racists*, 77.

20 Quoted in John Powell, *Racing to Justice*, 105.

21 Adam Liptak, "Race and College Admissions, Facing a New Test by Justices." http://www.nytimes.com/2012/10/09/us/supreme-court-to-hear-case-on-affirmative-action.html?_r=2&pagewanted=all&.Online. Accessed 1 April 2013.

22 Quoted in George Lipsitz, *The Possessive Investment in Whiteness*, 225.

23 Quoted in Stephen Steinberg, *Turning Back*, 168.

24 Michael Kinsley, "How Affirmative Action Helped George W." http://www.cnn.com/2003/ALLPOLITICS/01/20/timep.affirm.action.tm/index.html.Online. Accessed 1 April 2013.

25 Stephen Steinberg, *Turning Back*, 133.

26 Ibid, 117.

27 Ibid, 133.

Chapter 5

1   Howard Winant, "A Dream Deferred," 220.

2   Evelyn Nakano Glenn, "Consuming Lightness," 166.

3   Phil Hutchison, "The Political Economy of Colorblindness," 218.

4   Ibid.

5   Quoted in James W. Loewen, *Lies My Teacher Told Me*, 197.

6   James McPherson, *Abraham Lincoln and the Second American Revolution*, 19.

7   WEB DuBois, *Black Reconstruction in America*, 30.

8   Charles Lofgren, *The Plessy Case*, 244n8.

9   Mark Golub, "*Plessy* as 'Passing,'" 573.

10 Charles Lofgren, *The Plessy Case*, 173.

11 Mark Golub, "*Plessy* as 'Passing,'" 573.

12 Quoted in Mark Elliott, *Color-Blind Justice*, 6.

13 See Phil Hutchison, "The Political Economy of Colorblindness," chapter 1.

14 On this point, see Cheryl Harris, "Whiteness as Property" and George Lispitz, *The Possessive Investment in Whiteness*.

15 Quoted in Mark Elliott, *Color-Blind Justice*, 4.

16 See Mark Elliott, *Color-Blind Justice*.

17 Quoted in David W. Bishop, "Plessy v. Ferguson: A Reinterpretation," 125.

18 163 U.S. 549.

19 163 U.S. 550.

20 163 U.S. 544.

21 163 U.S. 552.

22 163 U.S. 551.

23 Mark Golub, "*Plessy* as 'Passing,'" 582.

24 163 U.S. 553.

25 163 U.S. 557, my emphasis.

26 163 U.S. 560, my emphasis.

27 163 U.S. 562, my emphasis.

28 163 U.S. 555.

29 163 U.S. 559.

30 163 U.S. 559.

31 On this point, see David Theo Goldberg, *The Racial State*; Neil Gotanda, "A Critique of 'Our Constitution Is Color-Blind'"; and Jack Balkin, "*Plessy, Brown*, and *Grutter*."

32 Reva Siegel, "The Racial Rhetorics of Colorblind Constitutionalism," 50, her emphases.

33 Joel Olson, *The Abolition of White Democracy*, 102.

34 Mary Frances Berry, "Vindicating Martin Luther King, Jr.," 138.

35 Peter Irons, *Jim Crow's Children*, 29.

36 Brook Thomas, *American Literary Realism and the Failed Promise of Contract*, 195.

37 Tinsley Yarbrough, *Judicial Enigma*, 226.

38 Thomas Holt, *Children of Fire*, 218-9.

39 Michael Klarman, *From Jim Crow to Civil Rights*, 22.

Chapter 6

1   Quoted in Tinsley Yarbrough, *Judicial Enigma*, 229.

2   Quoted in Eric Sundquist, *King's Dream*, 214.

3   Neil Foley, *Quest for Equality*, 111.

4   Scott Kurashige, *The Shifting Grounds of Race*, 235.

5   Ibid, 237.

6   See David Freund, *Colored Property*.

7   Scott Kurashige, *The Shifting Grounds of Race*, 235.

8   347 U.S. 494.

9   347 U.S. 495.

10 Mary Dudziak, *Cold War Civil Rights*; Matthew Lassiter, *The Silent Majority*, ch. 1.

11 Ralph Lee Smith, "The South's Pupil Placement Laws: Newest Weapon Against Integration." *Commentary*, October 1960.

12 Martin Luther King, Jr., *Where Do We Go from Here?*, 10.

13 349 U.S. 294.

14 Charles Silberman, *Crisis in Black and White*, 286.

15 Michelle Alexander, *The New Jim Crow*, 40.

16 Quoted in Matthew Lassiter, *The Silent Majority*,

17 Kenneth O'Reilly, *Nixon's Piano*, 292.

18 Quoted in ibid, 327, emphasis removed.

19 Quoted in Phil Hutchison, "The Political Economy of Colorblindness," 238.

20 Quoted in ibid.

21 Michael Flamm, *Law and Order*, 173.

22 Ibid.

23 Quoted in ibid, 1.

24 "Lee Atwater on the Southern Strategy." http://politicalwire.com/archives/ 2012/11/14/lee_atwater_on_the_southern_strategy.html.Online. Accessed 1 April 2013.

25 Nikhil Singh, "Racial Formation in an Age of Permanent War," 282.

26 Gary Blasi, "Advocacy Against the Stereotype," 45.

Chapter 7

1   Quoted in James Patterson, *Freedom Is Not Enough*, 124.

2   Ibid.

3   Ibid, 125.

4   Linda Faye Williams, *The Constraint of Race*, 179.

5   James Patterson, *Freedom Is Not Enough*, 125.

6   Linda Faye Williams, *The Constraint of Race*, 179.

7   Quoted in Kenneth O'Reilly, *Nixon's Piano*, 365.

8   Leslie Carr, *"Color-Blind" Racism*, 116.

9   Nikhil Singh, *Black Is a Country*, 42.

10 Phil Hutchison, "The Political Economy of Colorblindness," 203.

11 Nikhil Singh, *Black Is a Country*, 40.

12 "Images of Katrina and the Black Criminal: Finding vs. Looting" http://race
    .iheartsociology.com/2012/10/images-of-katrina-and-the-black-criminal-finding-
    vs-looting/Online. Accessed 1 April 2013.

13 Gary Blasi, "Advocacy Against the Stereotype," 46.

14 "Study: White and Black Children Biased Toward Lighter Skin." http://www.cnn
    .com/2010/US/05/13/doll.study/index.html.Online. Accessed 1 April 2013.

15 Jerry Kang, "Trojan Horses of Race," 125.

16 Ibid, 126.

17 Phil Hutchison, "The Political Economy of Colorblindness," 247.

18 Vijay Prashad, *Keeping Up with the (Dow) Joneses*, 84.

19 Michelle Alexander, *The New Jim Crow*, 130.

20 Gary Blasi, "Advocacy Against the Stereotype," 62-63.

21 Glenn Greenwald, *With Liberty and Justice for Some*, 111.

22 David Harvey, *The Enigma of Capital*, 1.

23 Ibid.

24 David Roediger, *How Race Survived U.S. History*, 229.

25 Ibid, 228, my emphasis.

26 Ibid, 229.

27 Ibid.

28 Gregory Squires and Charis Kubrin, *Privileged Places*, 56.

29 Ibid.

30 Beryl Satter, *Family Properties*, 373.

31 Ibid, 374.

32 Ibid.

33 Imani Perry, *More Beautiful and More Terrible*, 5-6.

34 Ibid, 128.

35 Martin Luther King, Jr., *Why We Can't Wait*, 17.

Conclusion

1 George Lipsitz, *The Possessive Investment in Whiteness*, 183.

2 See Richard Alba, *Blurring the Color Line*.

Works Cited

"Affirming Affirmative Action." *Los Angeles Times*. 16 August 2012.

Alba, Richard. *Blurring the Color Line: The New Chance for a More Integrated America*. Cambridge: Harvard University Press, 2009.

Alexander, Michelle. *The New Jim Crow: Mass Incarceration in the Age of Colorblindness*. New York, NY: The New Press, 2010.

Anderson, Elizabeth. *The Imperative of Integration*. Princeton: Princeton University Press, 2010.

Awkward, Michael. *Burying Don Imus: Anatomy of a Scapegoat*. Minneapolis, MN: University of Minnesota Press, 2009.

Balkin, Jack. "*Plessy, Brown*, and *Grutter*: A Play in Three Acts." *Cardozo Law Review 1689* 26 (2005), 101–41.

Berry, Mary Frances. "Vindicating Martin Luther King, Jr.: The Road to a Color-Blind Society." *The Journal of Negro History* 81:4 (Winter 1996), 137–44.

Bertrand, Marianne and Sendhil Mullainathan. "Are Emily and Greg More Employable than Lakisha and Jamal?: A Field Experiment on Labor Market Discrimination." *The American Economic Review* 94:4 (September 2004), 991–1013.

Bishop, David W. "Plessy v. Ferguson: A Reinterpretation." *The Journal of Negro History* 62:2 (1977), 125–33.

Blackmon, Douglas. *Slavery by Another Name: The Re-Enslavement of Black Americans from the Civil War to World War II*. Norwell, MA: Anchor Press, 2009.

Blasi, Gary. "Advocacy Against the Stereotype: Lessons from Cognitive Social Psychology." In Gregory Parks, Shayne Jones, and W. Jonathan Cardi, eds., *Critical Race Realism: Intersections of Psychology, Race, and Law*. New York, NY: The New Press, 2008, 45–65.

Bloom, Jack. *Class, Race, and the Civil Rights Movement: The Changing Political Economy of Southern Racism*. Bloomington, IN: Indiana University Press, 1987.

Bonilla-Silva, Eduardo. *Racism without Racists: Color-Blind Racism and the Persistence of Racial Inequality in the United States*, 3rd ed. Lanham, MD: Rowman and Littlefield, 2010.

Bonilla-Silva, Eduardo and David G. Embrick. "Are Blacks Color Blind Too?: An Interview-Based Analysis of Black Detroiters' Racial Views." *Race and Society* 4 (2001), 47–67.

Carmichael, Stokely and Charles V. Hamilton. *Black Power: The Politics of Liberation in America*. New York, NY: Vintage Books, 1967.

Carr, Leslie. *"Color-Blind" Racism*. Thousand Oaks, CA: Sage Publications, 1997.

Colby, Tanner. *Some of My Best Friends Are Black: The Strange Story of Integration in America*. New York, NY: Viking, 2012.

Cone, James. *Martin and Malcolm and America: A Dream or a Nightmare*. Maryknoll, NY: Orbis Books, 1992.

DuBois, WEB. *Black Reconstruction in America, 1860-1880*. New York, NY: Free Press, 1999.

Dudziak, Mary. *Cold War Civil Rights: Race and the Image of American Democracy*. Princeton, NJ: Princeton University Press, 2011.

Elliott, Mark. *Color-Blind Justice: Albion Tourgee and the Quest for Racial Equality from the Civil War to Plessy v. Ferguson*. New York, NY: Oxford University Press, 2008.

Elmelech, Yuval. *Transmitting Inequality: Wealth and the American Family*. Lanham, MD: Rowman and Littlefield, 2008.

Feagin, Joe R. *Systemic Racism: A Theory of Oppression*. New York, NY: Routledge, 2006.

Foley, Neil. *Quest for Equality: The Failed Promise of Black-Brown Solidarity*. Cambridge: Harvard University Press, 2010.

Fong, Timothy. *The Contemporary Asian American Experience*, 3rd ed. New York, NY: Prentice Hall, 2007.

Fredrickson, George. *Racism: A Short History*. Princeton: Princeton University Press,2003.

Freund, David MP. *Colored Properties: State Policy and White Racial Politics in Suburban America*. Chicago, IL: University of Chicago Press, 2008.

Gilens, Martin. *Why Americans Hate Welfare: Race, Media, and the Politics of Antipoverty Policy*. Chicago, IL: University of Chicago Press, 2000.

Glenn, Evelyn Nakano. "Consuming Lightness: Segmented Markets and Global Capital in the Skin Whitening Trade." In Evelyn Nakano Glenn, ed., *Shades of Difference: Why Skin Color Matters*. Stanford, CA: Stanford University Press, 2009, 166–87.

Goldberg, David Theo. *The Racial State*. Malden, MA: Blackwell, 2002.

Golub, Mark. "*Plessy* as 'Passing': Judicial Responses to Ambiguously Raced Bodies in *Plessy v. Ferguson*." *Law and Society Review* 39:3 (September 2005), 563–600.

Gotanda, Neil. "A Critique of 'Our Constitution Is Color-Blind.'" In Gary Peller, Kimberle Crenshaw, Neil Gotanda, and Kendall Thomas, *eds., Critical Race Theory: The Key Writings that Formed the Movement*. New York, NY: The New Press, 1995, 257–75.

Greenwald, Glenn. *With Liberty and Justice for Some: How the Law Is Used to Destroy Equality and Protect the Powerful*. New York, NY: Metropolitan Books, 2012.

Guinier, Lani and Gerald Torres. *The Miner's Canary: Enlisting Race, Resisting Power, Transforming Democracy*. Cambridge: Harvard University Press, 2002.

Haney-Lopez, Ian. "A Nation of Minorities: Race, Ethnicity, and Reactionary Colorblindness." *Stanford Law Review* 59 (February 2007), 985–1063.

Harris, Cheryl. "Whiteness as Property." *Harvard Law Review* 106 (1993), 1709–95.

Harvey, David. *The Enigma of Capital and the Crises of Capitalism.* Oxford: Oxford University Press, 2010.

Hayden, Dolores. *Building Suburbia: Green Fields and Urban Growth, 1820-2000.* New York, NY: Vintage, 2004.

Ikard, David and Martell Lee Teasley. *Nation of Coward: Black Activism in Barack Obama's Post-Racial America.* Bloomington, IN: Indiana University Press, 2012.

Irons, Peter. *Jim Crow's Children: The Broken Promise of the Brown Decision.* New York ,NY: Penguin, 2004.

Johnson, Heather Beth. *The American Dream and the Power of Wealth: Choosing Schools and Inheriting Inequality in the Land of Opportunity.* New York, NY: Routledge, 2006.

Kang, Jerry. "Trojan Horses of Race." In Gregory Parks, Shayne Jones, and W. Jonathan Cardi, eds., *Critical Race Realism: Intersections of Psychology, Race, and Law.* New York, NY: The New Press, 2008, 125–54.

Katz, Michael B. *The Undeserving Poor: From the War on Poverty to the War on Welfare.* New York, NY: Pantheon, 1990.

Katznelson, Ira. *When Affirmative Action Was White: An Untold History of Racial Inequality in Twentieth-Century America.* New York, NY: W. W. Norton, 2004.

Klarman, Michael. *From Jim Crow to Civil Rights: The Supreme Court and the Struggle for Racial Equality.* Oxford: Oxford University Press, 2004.

Kurashige, Scott. *The Shifting Grounds of Race: Black and Japanese Americans in the Making of Multiethnic Los Angeles.* Princeton, NJ: Princeton University Press, 2008.

Lassiter, Matthew. *The Silent Majority: Suburban Politics in the Sunbelt South.* Princeton, NJ: Princeton University Press, 2006.

Lawrence III, Charles R. and Mari Matsuda. *We Won't Go Back: Making the Case for Affirmative Action.* Boston, MA: Houghton Mifflin, 1997.

Lipsitz, George. *The Possessive Investment in Whiteness: How White People Profit from Identity Politics.* Philadelphia, PA: Temple University Press, 1998.

Lipsitz, George. "The Possessive Investment in Whiteness: Racialized Social Democracy and the 'White' Problem in American Studies." *American Quarterly* 47:3 (September 1995), 369–87.

Litwack, Leon. *How Free Is Free?: The Long Death of Jim Crow.* Cambridge: Harvard University Press, 2009.

Loewen, James W. *Lies My Teacher Told Me,* 2nd ed. New York, NY: Touchstone, 2007.

MacLean, Nancy. *Freedom is Not Enough: The Opening of the American Workplace.* Cambridge: Harvard University Press, 2006.

Massey, Douglas. *Categorically Unequal: The American Stratification System.* New York, NY: Russell Sage Foundation, 2007.

Massey, Douglas and Nancy Denton. *American Apartheid: Segregation and the Making of the Underclass.* Cambridge: Harvard University Press, 1998.

McPherson, James. *Abraham Lincoln and the Second American Revolution*. Oxford: Oxford University Press, 1992.

Mendelberg, Tali. *The Race Card: Campaign Strategy, Implicit Messages, and the Norm of Equality*. Princeton, NJ: Princeton University Press, 2001.

Mills, Charles W. "Modernity, Persons, and Subpersons." In Joseph Young and Jana Evans Braziel,eds., *Race and the Foundations of Knowledge: Cultural Amnesia in the Academy*. Chicago, IL: University of Illinois Press, 2006, 211–52.

Mills, Charles W. "Racial Exploitation and the Wages of Whiteness." In George Yancy, ed., *What White Looks Like: African American Philosophers on the Whiteness Question*. New York, NY: Routledge, 2004, 25–54.

Mills, Charles W. "White Supremacy as Sociopolitical System: A Philosophical Perspective." In Ashley W. Doane and Eduardo Bonilla-Silva, eds., *White Out: The Continuing Significance of Racism*. New York, NY: Routledge, 2003, 35–48.

Moynihan, Daniel Patrick. *The Negro Family: The Case for National Action*. Available at: http://www.dol.gov/oasam/programs/history/webid-meynihan.htm.

Oliver, Melvin and Thomas M. Shapiro. *Black Wealth/White Wealth: A New Perspective on Racial Inequality*, 2nd ed. New York, NY: Routledge, 2006.

Olson, Joel. *The Abolition of White Democracy*. Minneapolis, MN: University of Minnesota Press, 2004.

O'Reilly, Kenneth. *Nixon's Piano: Presidents and Racial Politics from Washington to Clinton*. New York, NY: Free Press, 1995.

Oshinsky, David M. *Worse Than Slavery: Parchman Farm and the Ordeal of Jim Crow Justice*. New York, NY: Free Press, 1997.

Pager, Devah. *Marked: Race, Crime, and Finding Work in an Era of Mass Incarceration*. Chicago, IL: University of Chicago Press, 2007.

Painter, Nell Irvin. *The History of White People*. New York, NY: W. W. Norton, 2010.

Perry, Imani. *More Beautiful and More Terrible: The Embrace and Transcendence of Racial Inequality in the United States*. New York, NY: New York University Press, 2011.

Powell, John A. *Racing to Justice: Transforming Our Conceptions of Self and Other to Build an Inclusive Society*. Bloomington, IN: Indiana University Press, 2012.

Prashad, Vijay. *Keeping Up with the (Dow) Joneses: Debt, Prison, Workfare*. Boston, MA: South End Press, 2003.

Rainwater, Lee and William Yancey. *The Moynihan Report and the Politics of Controversy*. Boston, MA: the MIT Press, 1967.

Rigney, Daniel. *The Matthew Effect: How Advantage Begets Further Advantage*. New York, NY: Columbia University Press, 2010.

Roberts, Dorothy. *Fatal Invention: How Science, Politics, and Big Business Re-Create Race in the Twenty-First Century*. New York, NY: The New Press, 2011.

Roediger, David. *How Race Survived U.S. History: From Settlement and Slavery to the Obama Phenomenon*. New York, NY: Verso, 2008.

Ryan, William. *Blaming the Victim*, 2nd ed. New York, NY: Vintage, 1976.

Satter, Beryl. *Family Properties: Race, Real Estate, and the Exploitation of Black Urban America*. New York, NY: Metropolitan Books, 2009.

Shapiro, Thomas M. *The Hidden Cost of Being African American: How Wealth Perpetuates Inequality*. Oxford: Oxford University Press, 2004.

Shapiro, Thomas M., Tatjana Meschede and Laura Sullivan. "The Racial Wealth Gap Increases Fourfold." Available at: http://iasp.brandeis.edu/pdfs/Author/shapiro-thomas-m/THE%20RACIAL%20WEALTH%20GAP%20INCREASES%20FOURFOLD.pdf

Siegel, Reva. "The Racial Rhetorics of Colorblind Constitutionalism: The Case of *Hopwood v. Texas*." In Robert Post and Michael Rogin, eds., *Race and Representation: Affirmative Action*. New York, NY: Zone Books, 1998, 29–73.

Silberman, Charles. *Crisis in Black and White*. New York, NY: Random House, 1964.

Singh, Nikhil Pal. *Black Is a Country: Race and the Unfinished Struggle for Democracy*. Cambridge: Harvard University Press, 2004.

Singh, Nikhil Pal. "Racial Formation in an Age of Permanent War." In Daniel Martinez HoSang, Oneka LaBennett, and Laura Pulido, eds., *Racial Formation in the Twenty-First Century*. Berkeley, CA: University of California Press, 2011, 276–301.

Sitkoff, Harvard. *The Struggle for Black Equality*, rev. ed. New York, NY: Hill and Wang, 2008.

Squires, Gregory and Charis Kubrin. *Privileged Places: Race, Residence, and the Structure of Opportunity*. Boulder, CO: Lynne Rienner, 2006.

Steinberg, Stephen. *The Ethnic Myth: Race, Ethnicity, and Class in America*, 2nd ed. Boston, MA: Beacon Press, 1989.

Steinberg, Stephen. *Turning Back: The Retreat from Racial Justice in American Thought and Policy*, 2nd ed. Boston, MA: Beacon Press, 2001.

Sugrue, Thomas. *The Origins of the Urban Crisis: Race and Inequality in Postwar Detroit*. Princeton, NJ: Princeton University Press, 2005.

Sullivan, Shannon. *Revealing Whiteness: The Unconscious Habits of Racial Privilege*. Bloomington, IN: Indiana University Press, 2006.

Sundquist, Eric J. *King's Dream*. New Haven, CT: Yale University Press, 2009.

Thomas, Brook. *American Literary Realism and the Failed Promise of Contract*. Berkeley, CA: University of California Press, 1997.

Tise, Larry E. *Proslavery: A History of the Defense of Slavery in America, 1701-1840*. Athens, GA: University of Georgia Press, 2004.

Williams, Linda Faye. *The Constraint of Race: Legacies of White Skin Privilege in America.* University Park, TX: The Pennsylvania State University Press, 2003.

Winant, Howard. "A Dream Deferred: Toward the U.S. Racial Future." In David Grusky and Tamar Kricheli-Katz, eds., *The New Gilded Age: The Critical Inequality Debates of Our Time.* Stanford, CA: Stanford University Press, 2012, 211–29.

Winant, Howard. *The New Politics of Race: Globalism, Difference, Justice.* Minneapolis, MN: University of Minnesota Press, 2004.

Winant, Howard. *The World Is a Ghetto: Race and Democracy Since World War II.* New York, NY: Basic Books, 2001.

Wu, Frank H. *Yellow: Race in America beyond Black and White.* New York, NY: Basic Books, 2002.